PEOPLE FOR the AMERICAN WAY FOUNDATION

HOSTILE CLIMATE

REPORT ON ANTI-GAY ACTIVITY • 1998 EDITION

Published by:
People For the American Way Foundation
2000 M Street, NW
Washington, D.C. 20036

First Printing June 1998
ISBN -1-890780-02-2

Printed in the United States of America

Dear Reader:

It would be easy to be dispirited about this accumulated evidence of anti-gay bigotry. As an American, it saddens me that so much energy is expended to demonize this part of our community. As a Christian, it angers me that the movement to deny equal rights to gay men and lesbians is led by politicians and political organizations that use the language of my faith to promote a hatred that is unlike anything I learned at home or at church.

I take heart from the fact that millions of Americans — I believe more than ever before — understand that core American values of fairness and equal opportunity are at stake in this struggle, and that our nation will be strengthened if we welcome gay and lesbian friends, family members, and neighbors as full partners.

Progress is being made at every level. Corporations are recognizing the benefits of treating gay and lesbian employees with fairness and respect. Local elected officials are affirming that anti-gay discrimination has no legitimate place in our public life. Courageous religious leaders and congregations are standing up for the gay and lesbian people in their communities.

We all know that there is no progress without struggle. It is important to document, analyze, and understand the outrages perpetrated against gays and lesbians in this country, as this report does. It is even more important to understand and act on the values that motivate us in this struggle. I want my grandchildren to grow and thrive in a society that offers them life, liberty and the pursuit of happiness, without exceptions based on whom they love. Let us understand the obstacles to that vision and do what we must to overcome them.

Carole Shields
President
People For the American Way Foundation
June 1998

EXECUTIVE SUMMARY

This document reports on a persistent wave of anti-gay activity centered in America's major institutions — business, government, the media, religious bodies, schools and universities and elsewhere. It covers incidents that occurred during 1997 and that were reported to or uncovered by People For the American Way Foundation researchers.

In a disturbingly large share of the incidents, the Religious Right political movement initiated the incident of intolerance, not surprising since the movement continues its steady anti-gay drumbeat in its communications with members and the public. That hostility extends far beyond opposing what the Right calls "special rights" for gays and lesbians, and includes outright anti-gay bigotry and prejudice, often uttered on national television or distributed in mass mailings.

Not all of the anti-gay activity can be laid at the feet of the Religious Right, however. A significant share of the incidents reported in these pages stems from simple institutional ignorance or indifference. In far too many instances, the major institutions of American society are unwilling to afford to gays and lesbians the protections they would routinely extend to other targeted minority groups.

The 170 incidents in this report are divided into six categories: employment, culture wars, marriage and family, education, religion, general intolerance. The data demonstrate that:

- **EMPLOYMENT.** Gay men and lesbians face outright discrimination in hiring, promotion and firing decisions. In most states it is perfectly legal to refuse to hire, to fire or to otherwise discriminate on the job on the basis of sexual orientation. In 1997, the absence of such anti-discrimination laws was keenly felt.

- **CULTURE WARS.** Religious Right leaders continued to attack the media for its occasional positive portrayals of gay and lesbian characters. Targets included the Disney entertainment empire and the comic strip, *For Better or For Worse.*

- **MARRIAGE AND FAMILY.** Committed partners of the same gender continued to be the subject of rampant discrimination in 1997, touching on such issues as marriage, adoption, foster parenting and more.

■ **EDUCATION.** Local public schools continue to face withering pressure from the Religious Right to eschew books and other curricular material that acknowledge homosexuality or that portray gay and lesbian characters in anything but a negative light. Similar controversies raged in university settings as well.

■ **RELIGION.** The institution many Americans turn to for lessons in compassion, decency and civility, too often turned its back on gay men and lesbians in 1997. Many houses of worship closed their doors to gay worshippers, and a number of religious groups called on Americans to exclude gay men and lesbians from the larger community.

■ **GENERAL INTOLERANCE.** A barrage of anti-gay rhetoric polluted America's civil discourse in 1997, as a variety of institutions or their leaders sought to demean their fellow citizens on the basis of sexual orientation. Such rhetoric all too frequently came from elected leaders.

The Hostile Climate that these various anti-gay activities create effectively denies gay men and lesbians full and open participation in American society. That is in fact the goal of the practitioners of bigotry. While some progress has been made in recent years as gay men and lesbians have become increasingly visible in popular culture, a long journey remains.

INTRODUCTION

Almost two and a quarter centuries ago, America was founded on a set of basic principles: Liberty. Equality. Opportunity. Fairness. Much of our history is a chronicle of the struggle to breathe life into these noble ideals. Dedicated leaders and citizens have worked to eliminate hate and prejudice, open up closed institutions, and give each individual the right to fulfill his or her potential. But it has not been easy. Progress has been slow and fitful. Racial minorities and women have struggled for equality, civil rights and fair treatment, and have been met with prejudice and bigotry. It seems all too easy for the majority to distance itself from those it sees as "different." Change has often been accompanied by acts of hate and violence against those who seek equality and fairness as well as against those who work on their behalf.

This fight for fairness is a difficult and painful one for lesbians and gay men.* Like African Americans, Latinos, and other racial minorities, gay men and lesbians face the grinding reality of prejudice and the all too real threat of hate-inspired violence. They must also deal with institutional bigotry and the resulting discrimination that persists in far too many of America's most prestigious institutions — at the highest level of government, in corporations, educational and religious institutions, the media and elsewhere. As long as distinguished organizations that should be standing for justice and fairness are the source of discrimination, disdain and division, the American ideal of tolerance and respect remains unfulfilled.

These institutions are still struggling with race and gender issues. For the most part, however, their leadership now conveys the message that blatant racist or sexist statements and actions are wrong and should not be tolerated. The report that follows documents the sad fact that this is not true for anti-gay behavior. Many powerful organizations do not consider prejudice and even hate directed against gay men and lesbians to be outrageous or unacceptable. Instead of working to promote the nation's basic values, key institutions too often project a hostile climate that nurtures division and discrimination.

---

* Nearly all of the incidents reported in Hostile Climate document activity targeting gay men or lesbians. In a few incidents, bisexual and trans-gendered individuals were included in the group targeted, e.g., action taken against a campus organization of gay, lesbian, bisexual and trans-gendered students. Therefore, we use the terms 'gay,' 'gay and lesbian,' and 'lesbian and gay' not to exclude bisexual and transgendered individuals from the discussion of prejudice based on sexual orientation, but to reflect, accurately, that the incidents reported to us involved almost exclusively lesbians and gay men. (We are aware, of course, that bisexual and transgendered individuals are often targets of prejudice and discrimination; the absence of reported incidents of this type does not mean such incidents are not occurring.) When transgendered or bisexual individuals were involved, that is indicated in the incident write-up.

This institutionalized intolerance does not just prevent the nation from realizing the dream of full and equal participation by all Americans in our national community. The incidents reported in *Hostile Climate* show how such intolerance also encourages anti-gay groups and individuals and makes it easier for them to spread prejudice. Such prejudice thrives, in large part, because large numbers of Americans are convinced they do not know a gay man or a lesbian. Given that, it is an easy task for leaders of the anti-gay movement to portray lesbians and gay men in negative ways that range from "different" to "monstrous." The goal, of course, is to create distance between gays and lesbians and the rest of the populace, to define them as something to fear, as enemies of families, of children, of the church. The Right knows that if lesbians and gay men "come out," if they reveal themselves where they are in every family, in every church, in every workplace, hearts and minds will change. And so the Right's steady drumbeat of fear and hatred is designed to prevent exactly that; it is designed to threaten those lesbians and gay men and keep them in the closet, to keep honest portrayals of their lives off of television and movie screens, and to keep "mainstream" Americans from discovering who their gay and lesbian daughters, sons, ministers, co-workers and neighbors are.

"Homosexuality is a vile perversion that if we leave unchecked will bring the downfall of the nation. . . .Homosexual marriage violates God's law. We need to outlaw homosexual activities in the state and enforce that law."

Founder of **Wisconsin Christians United** at a rally for Biblical morality and marriage in Wisconsin

This report, which covers activity in 1997, documents incidents that contribute to a climate that is hostile to an entire segment of the American populace. The information about these incidents comes from both primary sources — including phone interviews with those involved in the incidents — and secondary source materials. The secondary material includes newspapers, Internet reports, and newsletters and direct mail from anti-gay organizations.

Hostile Climate does not attempt to be an exhaustive compilation of the thousands of serious anti-gay incidents that took place in 1997. Other organizations do an excellent job of recording hate crimes, abuse and harassment. One, the National Gay and Lesbian Task Force, produces a comprehensive review of state legislation on lesbian and gay issues. This report focuses on actions by individuals, institutions, or government that have policy implications or set important precedents. *Hostile Climate* is, in fact, only a "snapshot" of anti-gay activity in the last year.

The story that this report tells, while complex, leads to a simple and tragic conclusion: In 1997, too many lesbians and gay men received a message of exclusion and rejection, and too many organizations continued to tolerate discrimination, prejudice and bigotry. *Hostile Climate* makes all too clear that the nation's leading institutions have a long way to go before they embody the values on which America was founded.

THE RELIGIOUS RIGHT'S ANTI-GAY CRUSADE

In 1997, the Religious Right continued its relentless assault on gay and lesbian people and those who advocate respect for gay and lesbian people. Religious Right groups filled the airways with hate-filled rhetoric, produced thousands of copies of venomous books, videos, and pamphlets, and crammed their websites with the worst kinds of stereotypes and vitriol.

When courageous officials and citizens call the Religious Right to account, their spokespersons often claim that they "hate the sin, but love the sinner." A close look at the rhetoric they use, however, tells a different story. The Religious Right does all it can to drown out any attempts to show that gay men and lesbians are human beings. Instead, Religious Right leaders define gay men and lesbians in terms of disease and depravity.

They also exploit these vicious stereotypes for cash. Religious Right groups blanket the country with anti-gay fundraising letters, plus video, radio, and website appeals. These are laden with mean-spirited caricatures of gays and lesbians and grotesque distortions of attempts to promote tolerance and equal treatment. With their blatant pandering to hate, Religious Right groups reap millions of dollars and recruit thousands of new members every year.

"[The comic page] should not be used as an indoctrination tool for the homosexual lifestyle. . . .homosexuality is immoral, unscriptural and unhealthy."

Don Jackson of the **Christian Family Network,** objecting to a gay theme in the comic strip *For Better or For Worse*

While the Religious Right's activities are the most disgusting examples of intolerance reported in these pages, it is important to keep in mind that they are a symptom of a larger problem. The leaders of the Religious Right choose the target of their attacks carefully, armed with the knowledge that major institutions are willing to ignore hostility toward gay people. They have made a cold political calculation: homophobia is one form of bigotry that can still be exploited without bringing down the wrath of "mainstream" America. It resonates widely because our nation's institutions are not doing enough to fight it.

In 1997, the fundraising appeals of Religious Right groups once again showed how far they were willing to go to dehumanize and demonize gay men and lesbians.

■ In April, Religious Right leader Pat Robertson attacked the city of San Francisco's requirement that businesses provide benefits to same-sex couples. "San Francisco is a cancer in the body politic . . .What [laws like San Francisco's] say is that we must enshrine sodomy, adultery and promiscuity into the law-code of the nation, enshrine it as a sacred right, not as aberrant behavior."

■ In June, Gary L. Bauer, president of the Religious Right Family Research Council wrote, "Those who practice homosexuality embrace a culture of death. They risk their lives as well as their mental and spiritual well-being. That is reason enough to discourage this practice. But now a band of radical activists, many of them highly placed, put the well being of all society at risk to satisfy their craving for approval."

■ "Vice President Al Gore has committed moral treason!" wrote Jerry Falwell. "He recently praised the lesbian actress who plays 'Ellen' on ABC Television . . .I believe he may even put children, young people, and adults in danger by his public endorsement of deviant homosexual behavior. . . Our elected leaders are attempting to glorify and legitimize perversion."

To fight efforts to teach tolerance in schools, in 1997 the Religious Right also trotted out one of its favorite tactics: accusing the gay rights movement of "recruiting" children to homosexuality.

■ The Family Research Council's Robert Knight said, "Homosexual activists have made such strides in gaining acceptance that now they feel the final frontier is the children. That's been the goal all along: get the next generation."

■ In June, Beverly LaHaye, Chairman of the Concerned Women of America, wrote in a fundraising letter, "Little children aren't sexually aware. God didn't intend them to be. Yet homosexuals are going into classes to strip children of their innocence and indoctrinate them."

Finally, Religious Right leaders grew bold enough to admit that they reject the entire notion of tolerance when gay men and lesbians are involved.

■ In a July fundraising letter, Robert Simonds, president of the National Association of Christian Educators/Citizens for Excellence in Education, wrote, "The word 'tolerance' was meant to soften up Christianity into accepting homosexuality as 'just another lifestyle.'"

When President Clinton addressed a fundraising dinner of the lesbian and gay civil rights group, the Human Rights Campaign, the Right had a field day attacking him for his message of tolerance and respect:

■ Andrea Sheldon of the Traditional Values Coalition, said, "If the American people are shocked by all of the same-sex smooching that is on television, wait until they see an American president kissing up to the wealthiest extremists of the amoral left."

■ Family Research Council's Robert Knight said, "To use the bully pulpit to glamorize behavior that offends the values of millions of Americans, behavior which is also unhealthy and destructive . . . is a disservice to the American people."

Perhaps the most significant recent action by the Religious Right has been the announcement by the Christian Coalition of its "Families 2000" project, a national campaign to rollback what few gains the lesbian and gay rights movement has made. "Families 2000" seeks the repeal of every anti-discrimination law or ordinance in the country that protects individuals discriminated against on the basis of sexual orientation. The project gained its first victory in the state of Maine. "Our Maine victory has set the stage to take this winning formula and apply it nationwide," Christian Coalition executive director Randy Tate said. "Our experience in Maine demonstrates the deep desire on the part of pro-family conservatives to take action on issues that directly affect their families and communities." The project also seeks the repeal of state gay adoption laws.

FINDINGS

As in previous reports, this year's edition of *Hostile Climate* begins with a discussion of our overall findings and an analysis of these findings, broken down by categories of incidents. The report then presents case studies of all the incidents we documented, organized under the same categories we use in this "Findings" section. We have included a map summarizing the number of incidents by state and an index so readers can locate the incidents by state as well.

People for the American Way Foundation's researchers documented 170 national, state, or local anti-gay incidents that demonstrate institutional bigotry and prejudice in 40 states, Puerto Rico and the District of Columbia during 1997. The breadth of this activity and its virulence overshadowed the important steps that were taken to end discrimination and intolerance.

We have analyzed the incidents of intolerance, grouping them into categories by the kind of institutions involved, the kinds of discrimination practiced, and the implications of the incidents on the daily lives of gay men and lesbians. The categories include:

■ **EMPLOYMENT**   ■ **CULTURE WARS**
■ **MARRIAGE AND FAMILY**   ■ **EDUCATION**
■ **RELIGION**   ■ **GENERAL INTOLERANCE**

EMPLOYMENT

As they struggled for the same rights and protections afforded to other Americans, gay men and lesbians continued to face a major battle in the workplace in 1997. The opponents of tolerance once again made an impact by arguing against so-called "special rights" for homosexuals. One clear indicator of the power of this argument is that some 40 states allow people to be fired simply because they are gay or lesbian, even though polls demonstrate that most Americans believe employment discrimination on the basis of sexual orientation is wrong.

During the year, supporters of equality and fairness worked to show that the real issues have nothing to do with "special rights." Being allowed to make a living and receive the same employment benefits all Americans do is not special treatment for gay men and lesbians. It is equal treatment for all of our citizens. Fair-minded people struggled to make their voices heard against the attacks of the Religious Right and the indifference or hostility of some of the nation's most prestigious institutions.

One of the Right's favorite tactics in distorting discussion of equal employment rights is the characterization of the quest for such rights by gay men and lesbians as a ploy to establish quotas and affirmative action programs. In spite of the fact that no anti-discrimination bill requires quotas and the federal Employment Non-Discrimination Act explicitly prohibits them, anti-gay leaders continue to raise the specter of gay employees being forced on business owners, and employees being required to work next to "radical homosexuals," even in churches. In fact, ENDA (and most other anti-discrimination laws) exempt churches and religious organizations.

In the military, gays and lesbians continued to face verbal and physical harassment as well as discrimination. The Servicemembers Legal Defense Network (SLDN) reported that military commanders routinely violate the Pentagon's "don't ask, don't tell" policy by aggressively investigating the private lives of military personnel suspected of being gay. SLDN found that violations of the policy rose from 443 in 1996 to 563 in 1997. Court challenges to the policy failed, and there were harrowing incidents of violence against gay sailors. Even Defense Secretary William Cohen acknowledged that "some commanders haven't gotten the message" about the administration's policy barring the pursuit and harassment of homosexuals in the military.

In civilian life, gay and lesbian workers continued to struggle to receive the rights and protections afforded to other Americans. They were opposed not only by the Religious Right, but by corpo-

"Because of Wilson's veto, private citizens won't be forced to open their homes, schools, businesses, and community organizations to gay activists who want to push their lifestyle on the rest of us."

Response of the **Capitol Resource Institute** to California Governor Pete Wilson's failure to sign a bill providing anti-discrimination protections to lesbians and gay men

rations, trade associations, county commissioners, city councils, and county Human Relations Commissions. Even the U.S. Congress joined by continuing to deny the District of Columbia funds to implement a 1992 domestic partners law. Too many of the nation's key institutions failed to promote the nation's basic values of opportunity, equality, and fairness.

- The U.S. Supreme Court again refused to hear a challenge to the "don't ask, don't tell" policy, this time in a case brought by a former Air Force captain who argued that the policy violated his free-speech rights and fostered government "discrimination and bigotry."

- The Navy discharged a top enlisted man for listing himself as gay on an online computer service. When the sailor sued for reinstatement, a federal judge ruled in his favor and called the Navy's investigation a "search and destroy mission."

- California governor Pete Wilson refused to sign a bill that would have added "sexual orientation" to the list of classes protected under the state's Fair Employment and Housing Acts. Instead he returned the bill to the legislature without signature, calling it "unnecessary."

- In Los Angeles, California a gay man who was the victim of escalating on-the-job harassment due to his sexual orientation was terminated from Anheuser-Busch. The employee had been told by plant management, "To tell co-workers that you are gay is unbecoming to a manager and will result in your termination."

- The Air Transport Association (ATA) filed a lawsuit in U.S. District Court in San Francisco marking one of the most significant challenges to San Francisco's pioneering requirement that all businesses contracting with the city extend the same benefits to unmarried employees' domestic partners that they do to married employees' spouses.

- Without public discussion, Dade County, Florida commissioners voted down a measure that would have prohibited discrimination against gay men and lesbians by amending the county's human rights ordinance that already banned discrimination on the basis of race, gender, and other characteristics.

- A Mitchell County, North Carolina sheriff ordered the illegal taping of phone conversations that led to the resignation of the local high school football coach, a gay man.

CULTURE WARS

While Religious Right groups have fought long and hard to convey negative images of gays and lesbians, they became more desperate and vehement in 1997. Despite its best efforts, the Religious Right was confronted with the fact that "mainstream" media — especially motion pictures and television — were becoming more tolerant of gay men and lesbians and more willing to depict them realistically and even sympathetically. In response, Religious Right groups put pressure on the media to prevent balanced images in movie and television.

"Proponents of ENDA fail to acknowledge that the homosexuals already have equal rights in the workplace. The American people overwhelmingly oppose a new federal law that will enshrine special rights for homosexuals."

Robert Knight of the **Family Research Council,** objecting to the Employment Non-Discrimination Act (ENDA), which would provide protections against job discrimination to lesbians and gay men

To censor positive images of gay men and lesbians, Religious Right groups launched ferocious campaigns against The Walt Disney Company. Disney was targeted in part because Ellen DeGeneres's character on ABC's "Ellen" came out in a highly rated episode. ABC is owned by Disney, but conservatives also objected to other Disney movies and the fact that the company provided employment benefits to its own employees.

While the controversy over "Ellen" and the Walt Disney Company generated headlines, many other instances of attempted and successful censorship of art with gay themes and against gay artists took place out of the public spotlight. Once again, the hostility to tolerance was not confined to the Religious Right. Sadly, city and county governments, schools, libraries and newspapers censored artistic works — including a Pulitzer prize-winning play and even one of the nation's most popular comic strips — that tried to portray gays and lesbians in non-stereotypical ways.

- The Southern Baptist Convention voted to boycott the Walt Disney Company and urged each of its 15.6 million members to withhold at least $100 a year they might have otherwise spent on Disney theme parks, movies, or merchandise. The boycott was initiated because of the Baptists' view that Disney had moved away from "enriching, family entertainment" and their belief that Disney's fair treatment of its lesbian and gay employees constituted anti-Christian bigotry.

- The personal and on-air 'coming out' of comedian Ellen DeGeneres and her television character "Ellen" caused an uproar among the Religious Right. The right-wing Media Research Center ran a full page advertisement in *Variety* denouncing the program as a "blatant attempt by Disney, ABC and 'Ellen' to promote homosexuality to America's families." Pat

Robertson (Christian Coalition), Phyllis Schlafly (Eagle Forum) and Jerry Falwell were among those Religious Right leaders who signed the 'open letter' condemning the episode as a "slap in the face to America's families." By year's end, some ABC affiliates complained that the show's content had driven away local advertisers, particularly those in the South. One ABC affiliate, WBMA in Birmingham, Alabama, refused to air the controversial episode.

■ The Universal Press–syndicated comic strip, *For Better or For Worse*, was censored from at least 30 daily newspapers for a series of cartoons dealing with the romantic concerns of a gay teenage character. Three newspapers canceled the strip altogether.

■ A private school in Corvallis, Oregon canceled a scheduled performance by a lesbian duo after concert promoters refused to edit promotional material referring to the singers as "life partners."

■ The San Antonio, Texas city council zeroed out funding for the Esperanza Peace and Justice Center, which sponsors the city's annual lesbian and gay film festival as part of the Center's diverse cultural programming.

MARRIAGE AND FAMILY

In the last decade, the term "family values" has become one of the Religious Right's favorite rhetorical weapons. Religious Right groups try to broaden their influence by claiming their goal is simply to protect the family. They also try to marginalize opponents with an "anti-family" label. However, the campaign to deny gay men and lesbians the same marriage and adoption rights and protections that other Americans enjoy shows that "family values" is a stark example of what George Orwell called "doublespeak." The Religious Right uses the term to promote hate, not the loving and caring that build stronger families.

Far from supporting or encouraging the loving families established by gay men and lesbians, the Religious Right's 1997 literature, speeches, radio shows, and demonstrations fomented hatred against them. And the radical groups did not stop there. In their attacks on gay and lesbian marriage and adoption rights, the Religious Right encouraged families to exclude their gay and lesbian members—weakening, not strengthening, family bonds.

To promote their exclusionary and intolerant version of family values, Religious Right spokespeople also argue that sanctioning committed gay and lesbian relationships is an attack on traditional heterosexual marriage. No proof or explanation of this claim is ever offered. As recently as the 1960s, similar arguments were used against sanctioning interracial marriages. Gay men and lesbians are asking only to share the rights, protections, obligations and benefits that accompany civil marriage, not weaken or destroy them.

Unfortunately, the Religious Right attacks were met with enthusiasm in far too many of the nation's important institutions and provided ammunition for too many conservative legislators. While gay men and lesbians won some victories in the courts on marriage and adoption rights, there were also some serious setbacks in 1997. The National Gay and Lesbian Task Force Policy Institute reported that 46 laws prohibiting same-sex unions were introduced around the country, ten of which were signed into law. Many local authorities continued to be hostile to adoption by gay and lesbian parents.

Moreover, almost every court case or local government decision that came to public notice, whatever the outcome, led to an outpouring of intolerant rhetoric and activity. The rhetoric, including stereotypes and specious claims about the dangers of gay parenting, came both from the Religious Right and from members of mainstream institutions — religious spokespersons, legislators, and government officials.

■ A Broward County, Florida lesbian couple was unsuccessful in their attempt to overturn a state law banning adoptions by lesbians and gay men. Their attorney argued that the 20-year ban violated the state constitution's guarantee of equal protection because the legislature was trying to exclude an entire group of the state's citizens from being adoptive parents.

- The Roman Catholic Archdiocese of Chicago was quick to attack a 5-2 vote by the Oak Park, Illinois village board to adopt a domestic partners registry. The Archdiocese released a statement on the day of the vote: "[T]he archdiocese affirms its conviction that heterosexual marriage and family life is an essential building block of a healthy and well-ordered society," the statement read. "As such, it deserves to be both promoted and protected by public policy. Such protection implies, of its very nature, that no other social realities will be granted equivalent status."

- A state senator expressed outrage when the Kentucky Court of Appeals ruled 2-to-1 that same-sex couples are covered by the state's domestic violence statute. Earlier in the year, the senator had stated, "We need to remember that activities which many heterosexuals would consider aberrant forms of violent behavior, such as sadomasochism, seem to be more accepted in the homosexual subculture."

- An organization of lesbian, gay, and bisexual parents, their children and friends was initially barred from participating in a community fundraising program sponsored by a Northampton, Massachusetts McDonald's franchise. Valuable Families had received an invitation to participate in the community "Food, Folks, and Fundraising" program where organization members staff the restaurant to raise money. Soon after they arranged an event at the restaurant, the franchise manager contacted the board chair of Valuable Families to say that McDonald's would not "allow" the organization to participate in an event at the restaurant because the organization was "too controversial."

- A member of the Puerto Rico House of Representatives filed a bill to amend the island's civil code to ban same-sex unions. The author of the bill claimed it would "make it very clear to homosexuals that this society does not tolerate their conduct....This is a question of defending the morals and the values we are teaching our children."

- A gay couple was barred from holding their commitment ceremony at a University of Tennessee campus chapel in Chattanooga, Tennessee.

- A Child Protective Services (CPS) employee in Dallas, Texas went to battle against the agency over its placement of foster children with lesbians and gay men.

EDUCATION

America has long relied on its public schools not only to convey knowledge but to impart the basic values of diversity, equality, and fairness while nurturing students' creativity and individuality. In 1997, however, actions by the Religious Right, state legislators, and even school officials too often turned school districts into battlefields and created a climate that was hostile to those values.

Religious Right groups used all the weapons in their arsenal — including lawsuits, organized demonstrations at school board meetings, letter writing campaigns, and talk radio — to wage war against any kind of classroom material or activity that tried to promote tolerance toward gay people. They targeted books, videotapes, discussions, presentations, and even posters. A favorite tactic was to label attempts to teach fairness as "recruitment" and "indoctrination," and then make the argument that libraries should "balance" pleas for tolerance with publications that stigmatize and stereotype gay people. (Of course, no institution would ever consider "balancing" arguments for racial tolerance with racist literature.)

Education officials too often failed to stand up for fair treatment. School administrators ignored the harassment of gay students. Boards of education voted against including sexual orientation in the list of categories protected from harassment or prohibited the formation of lesbian and gay student organizations. Higher education was not exempt, either. State legislators tried to stop funding of clubs for gay students and for academic programs that included gay-oriented subjects.

These actions by the Religious Right as well as by educational institutions that should have defended tolerance sent a painful message again and again to gay and lesbian young people: You are abnormal and should hate yourself. Heterosexual students received a dangerous message, too: Gays and lesbians are one minority that it's okay to hate.

It's not surprising, therefore, that the hostile climate in educational institutions was accompanied by a disturbing increase in anti-gay hate crimes in schools and colleges. According to the National Coalition of Anti-Violence Programs (NCAVP), such crimes increased 34 percent in 1997.

■ In an August 1997 fundraising letter, Concerned Women for America (CWA) attacked *It's Elementary: Teaching About Gay Issues in School* for "methodically break[ing] down children's natural resistance to accepting homosexuality as normal" and promoting "ungodly and immoral behavior that leads to death." The film is an award-winning documentary about the discussion of gay and lesbian issues in classrooms, intended for adults and sometimes used in teacher training. It incurred the wrath of Religious Right groups who denounced it as an effort to infiltrate schools for the purpose of "cynically recruiting a new generation to become homosexuals." Focus on the Family's "Current Issues of Concern" castigated the

National Endowment for the Arts' involvement in funding the "so-called educational film that is a brazen attempt to promote homosexuality to America's schoolchildren."

■ An Alabama state senator threatened to challenge funding for the University of Alabama at Tuscaloosa's Women's Studies program, unless administrators addressed his concerns over the program. "They are promoting sex between women," he charged. The department offered courses on topics such as women in the workplace, women and law, and women in the civil rights movement. Some classes have required reading lists that include lesbian issues and/or books authored by lesbian writers.

■ The Faculty Council of Idaho State University in Pocatello sued the Idaho Board of Education for violating the First Amendment after the board denied a state university history professor a research grant because his subject matter was deemed too controversial. His proposed project was an exploration of the history of lesbians and gay men in the Pacific northwest at the turn of the century. The faculty council passed a resolution saying that the denial was motivated by "an anticipated negative public reaction to funding a project dealing with homosexuality," and "produces a chilling effect on academic freedom."

■ The Wayne-Westland, Michigan community school board voted 6-1 to rescind its earlier vote adding "sexual orientation" to the list of classes protected from harassment in the district's code of conduct. The school board had previously voted to extend protection to lesbian and gay students and faculty. The school board president, a lesbian, then lost her re-election bid after anonymous inflammatory anti-gay fliers — titled "Take a Hike Dyke" — claimed she would introduce gay themes and topics into the curriculum.

■ A 1996 graduate filed a federal lawsuit charging anti-gay harassment at the Sussex County, New Jersey high school he attended. The lawsuit charged that neither the board of education nor teachers and administrators at Jefferson High School did anything to stop the anti-gay harassment after it was brought to their attention.

RELIGION

Most Americans take it for granted that they can worship at the church of their choice, share in all of its activities, and become part of its nurturing community. Most gay men and lesbians face a very different situation. Far too many are excluded from houses of worship unless they keep themselves closeted.

Sometimes this exclusion stems from a particular interpretation of scripture. Sometimes gay people are denied the comforts of religion simply because religious leaders are unwilling to take heed of their congregation's desire for tolerance and acceptance. Too often it is caused by organized pressure from the Religious Right, which can be counted on to oppose any church's attempt to treat gay people fairly.

In 1997, the Religious Right railed against churches and church leaders who pressed for fairness and acceptance, making churches that allowed the performance of same-sex marriages a special target. Around the country, church elders also continued to deny leadership positions and even membership to gay men and lesbians. Gay clergy lost their jobs. For gay people, houses of worship, which should be a source of love, comfort, and understanding, conveyed a message of rejection and hostility.

■ Right-wing groups including Americans for Truth about Homosexuality (AFTH) and the Family Research Council (FRC) protested a White House visit by openly gay Reverend Troy Perry (Metropolitan Community Church), dismissing the church's gay-affirming congregational message and claiming that the visit "further degrades the Office of the Presidency." Rev. Perry was one of some 120 religious leaders honored during an ecumenical breakfast at the White House.

■ Emory University in Atlanta, Georgia approved the performing of same-sex commitment ceremonies in its campus chapels, but enacted conditions on the new policy to make it more difficult for gays and lesbians to use the chapels. "They'll have to jump through more hoops," said an attorney for a gay couple denied access. "What [University officials] are choosing to do is discriminate against gays and lesbians."

■ A Lutheran pastor in Ames, Iowa was barred from his ministry because, although church doctrine accepts his sexual orientation, he acknowledged being in a committed same-sex relationship.

■ Church elders prohibited a performer from singing at a holiday concert in a Redwood Falls, Minnesota church due to the man's sexual orientation. The gay man had been scheduled to sing at the Christmas Eve service at the Redwood Falls Church of Christ. The man had been baptized in the church and grew up in the community. The church — not affiliated with the "open and affirming" United Church of Christ denomination — has a policy against gay men and lesbians in leadership positions.

GENERAL INTOLERANCE

When hate-filled words are spoken by isolated extremists and bigots, the rhetoric is offensive and can even be dangerous at times. But when spokespeople for prestigious institutions — such as businesses, community organizations, local governments, or law enforcement — spread intolerance they reinforce the barriers that prevent gay people from attaining equal rights and fair treatment. When such words are joined with intolerant actions, they keep America from being a community that cherishes diversity and extends fairness and opportunity to all its citizens.

Unfortunately, there was no shortage of intolerant speech and action by community leaders in 1997, reinforcing the hostile climate that lesbians and gay men face. Intolerance extended from local government to the floor of the U.S. Senate. Mayors, city councils, heads of businesses, and police officials lashed out at gay people. Conservative senators launched harsh attacks on an openly gay man nominated by President Clinton to be Ambassador to Luxembourg. Once again, the Religious Right exploited this institutional acceptance of intolerance to keep spreading its messages of hate. Its greatest success came in early 1998, when Maine voters overturned a state measure barring discrimination against gays and lesbians in employment, housing, public accommodations and credit. After that vote, the executive director of the Christian Coalition, said, "Our Maine victory set the stage to take this winning formula and apply it nationwide." He then announced the launch of "Families 2000," the vicious campaign to repeal anti-discrimination protections wherever they have been enacted.

"Lesbian love, sodomy are viewed by God as being detestable and abominable. Civil magistrates are to put people to death who practice these things."

Host of radio talk show in
Costa Mesa, California

Finally, the most shocking results of the hostile climate in 1997 were acts of violence and terrorism against the gay and lesbian community: the bombing of a lesbian nightclub in Atlanta, credit for which was claimed by "The Army of God"; an arson incident targeting a Norfolk, Virginia gay couple; and shotgun blasts fired into a gay bar in rural Pennsylvania.

■ President Clinton's nomination of an openly gay man, James C. Hormel, as U.S. Ambassador to Luxembourg drew fire from conservative members of Congress. A spokesman for one Republican senator said, "We just don't want the Senate's agreement to this nomination to be seen as agreement to a pro-gay rights agenda."

■ During a television broadcast, the chairman of Alabama Gov. Fob James's re-election campaign, long-time Montgomery, Alabama mayor Emory Folmar, used a disparaging term for homosexuals. "I used the word 'queer' and I'll use it again," Folmar said in response to criticism. "I'm not going to call them gay. I don't approve of their lifestyle one bit."

■ Five weeks after the double bombing of a local family planning clinic, an Atlanta, Georgia lesbian nightclub was rocked by an explosion, spraying four-inch nails and shrapnel into the crowd. Five patrons were injured. A second bomb was found in a backpack lying in a adjacent parking lot. Soon after the bombing, four Atlanta media outlets received letters claiming that the bombings of the women's health clinic and lesbian nightclub were carried out by "Units of The Army of God." The letters exclaimed, "We will target sodomites, there [sic] organizations and all those who push there [sic] agenda."

■ A special "people's veto" referendum in early 1998 gave Maine the dubious distinction of being the first state to nullify previously enacted state-wide provisions barring discrimination against gays and lesbians in employment, housing, public accommodations and credit.

■ Conservative Jewish groups and anti-gay activists protested the recognition of lesbians and gay men in the new Museum of Jewish Heritage, a New York City museum honoring survivors of the Holocaust, even filing a lawsuit to stop its September opening.

■ The Orangetown, New York Republican Committee removed an incumbent town board member from its November slate of candidates because of her involvement with local chapters of Parents, Families and Friends of Lesbians and Gays (PFLAG) and her volunteer work with a support organization that provides hot meals to homebound people with AIDS.

■ Mecklenburg County, North Carolina commissioners ousted their chairman because of his support for a gay political candidate.

■ The mayor of Myrtle Beach, South Carolina joined local business and religious leaders in attacking a statewide gay group and its plans for an April 1998 pride festival.

THE ROAD AHEAD

This report documents the fact that in 1997 gay men and lesbians still had to struggle against a hostile climate that prevents our country from making its noble ideals real. Moreover, the forces that whip up and sustain that climate are not weakening. Far from it.

But *Hostile Climate* also documents some hopeful signs of success in the struggle to extend tolerance, respect, and fairness to all Americans. These pages document how some teachers, administrators, school boards, libraries and local governments stood up for tolerance. Courts upheld the workplace and family rights of lesbians and gay men. Police officers and other government officials were punished for anti-gay actions. The lead character in a mainstream television show, and the actor who plays her, came out on national television. President Clinton and Vice President Gore spoke at gay rights fundraisers. An openly gay clergyman was invited to the White House.

These success stories show that when dedicated Americans are willing to work to build broad community coalitions and convey a clear message that appeals to the nation's commitment to tolerance, they can begin to open up closed institutions . . . even in a very hostile climate.

But the Religious Right is using noxious stereotypes and blatant appeals to intolerance to expand its reach. Homophobic themes are a staple of the materials it relies on to raise millions of dollars and recruit new members. If anything, Religious Right groups have stepped up their gay and lesbian bashing as some parts of the "mainstream" media show signs of more tolerant treatment, and as more Americans become comfortable with their own lesbian and gay loved ones and begin to stand up for fairness and equality.

So the battle wages on. Progress will come as more Americans stand up to bigotry and hate, and say no to the message of the Religious Right and their friends in the legislatures and on the courts. Our nation will become less hostile as its institutions — its churches and businesses, its governing bodies and schools, its communities and organizations — see lesbian and gay Americans as human beings and afford them the fair and equal treatment they deserve.

INCIDENT MAP

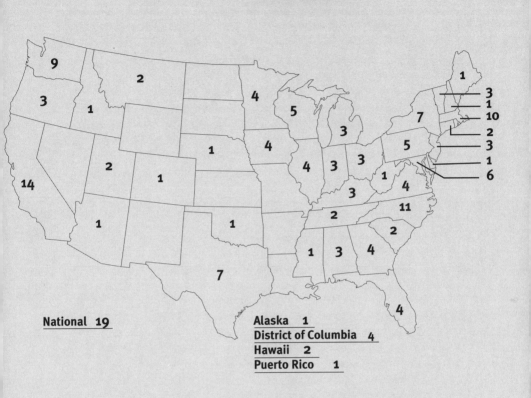

National 19

Alaska 1
District of Columbia 4
Hawaii 2
Puerto Rico 1

Alaska (1)
Alabama (3)
Arizona (1)
California (14)
Colorado (1)
Connecticut (2)
Delaware (1)
District of Columbia (4)
Florida (4)
Georgia (4)
Hawaii (2)
Idaho (1)
Illinois (4)
Indiana (3)

Iowa (4)
Kentucky (3)
Maine (1)
Maryland (6)
Massachusetts (10)
Michigan (3)
Minnesota (4)
Mississippi (1)
Montana (2)
Nebraska (1)
New Hampshire (1)
New Jersey (3)
New York (7)
North Carolina (11)

Ohio (3)
Oklahoma (1)
Oregon (3)
Pennsylvania (5)
Puerto Rico (1)
South Carolina (2)
Tennessee (2)
Texas (7)
Utah (2)
Vermont (3)
Virginia (4)
Washington (9)
West Virginia (1)
Wisconsin (5)

EMPLOYMENT

The issue of anti-discrimination protections for gay men and lesbians in the workplace continued to be controversial in 1997. Although employment discrimination is the most common complaint received by the American Civil Liberties Union from gay men and lesbians, the Religious Right continues to claim that gay men and lesbians are never discriminated against, that discrimination protections would constitute "special rights," and that gay men and lesbians have higher incomes than heterosexuals and thus have no need of legal protections. These allegations distort the facts, but they serve the Right well in its attempt to deny lesbians and gay men the right to be treated fairly in the workplace.

The proposed federal Employment Non-Discrimination Act (ENDA), defeated in a 1996 Senate vote of 50 - 49, was re-introduced in early 1997. The legislation would provide protection against employment discrimination based on sexual orientation at businesses with more than 15 employees, but it would not apply to the military or religious entities.

The Senate Labor and Human Resources Committee heard testimony in October on the proposed legislation. Five of the 18-member committee — four Democratic senators and committee chair, Sen. James Jeffords (R-VT) — attended the hearings. The committee is evenly split on ENDA; the eight Democratic committee members and Sen. Jeffords support the bill.

During the hearings, the senators heard from a restaurant worker who had a promotion rescinded after a co-worker told management she did not want to work with the employee because he is gay. The general manger told the employee "his sexual orientation was 'not compatible with [the restaurant chain]'s belief in family values,' and being gay had certainly destroyed [his] chances of becoming a manager."

In another incident, an attorney told the committee how his chances for employment were lost when he announced he was gay during the job interview with the Mesa, Arizona city prosecutor; he testified the prosecutor's "face fell and the tenor of the conversation completely changed" after he "came out."

"If the American people are shocked by all of the same-sex smooching that is on television, wait until they see an American president kissing up to the wealthiest extremists of the amoral left."

Andrea Sheldon of the **Traditional Values Coalition**, commenting on President Clinton's address to the Human Rights Campaign's fundraising dinner

Representatives from large corporations and small businesses alike testified in favor of ENDA. The chairman/CEO of Bell Atlantic said, "It is good business, and it is good citizenship." A small business owner testified, "We do not fear an explosion in litigation with ENDA."

Family Research Council president Gary Bauer called the testimony "one of the most one-sided proceedings I've ever seen." He claimed that "the committee didn't listen to those who have been victimized by so-called tolerance laws, people who lost their jobs because they object to the homosexual political agenda."

Chairman Jeffords reported that he was surprised that no one testified in opposition to the bill. "My staff scoured the country for witnesses with differing opinions, to no avail," he said. "Even those who had expressed a desire to testify [against the bill] changed their minds."

Not so, according to Family Research Council Director of Cultural Studies Robert Knight. "Proponents of ENDA fail to acknowledge that homosexuals already have equal rights in the workplace. The American people overwhelmingly oppose a new federal law that will enshrine special rights for homosexuals." [In dramatic contrast to FRC's claims, a survey conducted for The Associated Press in 1996 found that 85% of Americans believe gay people "should have equal rights in terms of job opportunities" and a *Newsweek* poll that same year showed 84% of Americans *support* workplace protections for gay men and lesbians.]

According to Knight, ENDA would cover "everything from foot fetishes to starring in gay porn films." Right-wing opponents have long claimed that ENDA would result in forced hiring of gay men and lesbians. But Jeffords said that the current version of ENDA precludes the Equal Employment Opportunity Commission (EEOC) from entering into a consent decree that includes quotas, or gives preferential treatment based on sexual orientation.

A spokesman for the Log Cabin Republicans — a gay Republican group — said that his organization has made ENDA a priority and its members have been meeting with fellow Republicans to build support for ENDA. Said the spokesman: "The strategy has shifted since the vote [in '96] ... took place," he said. "Now the strategy is to bring swing Republicans onto this bill."

President Clinton has indicated his firm endorsement of ENDA.

The number of gay men and lesbians facing discrimination in the military has risen for the fourth consecutive year, despite the Clinton administration's pledge to prevent further harassment in the armed forces.

According to a report issued by the Servicemembers Legal Defense Network (SLDN), military commanders routinely violate the Pentagon's "don't ask, don't tell" policy by aggressively investigating the private lives of military personnel suspected of being gay.

SLDN, which provides legal assistance to victims — heterosexual and homosexual — of the military's excesses in purportedly implementing the "don't ask, don't tell" policy, described the policy violations as "heavy handed and increasingly intrusive investigative tactics against suspected gays, including coercion and fishing expeditions," and reported that violations of the policy by the military rose from 443 in 1996 to 563 in 1997. SLDN also commented that there "is no recourse or redress for servicemembers asked, pursued or harassed," and those who violate the policy are not held accountable for their actions.

"The violations we are seeing are very basic," said one SLDN official. "[T]hey should not be occurring five years into the policy. Don't ask means don't ask. The rule could not be more clear, but time and again, investigating officers ask."

According to SLDN, there was a 39 percent increase in "Don't Question" violations since 1996, a 23 percent increase in "Don't Pursue" violations, and a 38 percent increase in "Don't Harass" violations. The Navy was the worst service offender, with 193 violations.

There was also significant activity in 1997 on the following fronts regarding the military's policy on gay men and lesbians:

■ In October, the U. S. Supreme Court again refused to hear a challenge to the "don't ask, don't tell" policy, this time in a case brought by a former Air Force captain who argued that the policy violated his free-speech rights and fostered government "discrimination and bigotry."

■ A three-judge panel of the 9th Circuit U.S. Court of Appeals ruled 2-1 that the policy does not violate the equal protection, due process, or free speech rights of gay servicemembers because the policy "does not distinguish between persons of homosexual and heterosexual orientation." The policy, said the court, provides that any person who makes a statement of homosexual orientation is subject to the same rebuttable presumption that they will engage in sex with a person of the same gender — irrespective of whether that person is homosexual or heterosexual.

■ In other cases, the 4th and 8th Circuits have upheld the military's policy.

■ At their annual convention in Salt Lake City, Utah, the Veterans of Foreign Wars voted to push the federal government to repeal the "don't ask, don't tell" policy and re-enact a blanket ban against gays in the military.

■ At the sexual misconduct trial of the Army's top enlisted man, defense lawyers tried to portray one accuser as unreliable on the grounds that she is a lesbian.

■ One week before he could receive his 20-year pension, the military discharged a decorated Army lieutenant colonel for being gay.

■ SLDN's report documented a series of incidents on the aircraft carrier *Eisenhower* over a two-month period last year, and called them a "most harrowing set of cases." In one case, a sailor was knocked unconscious by an assailant who addressed him with a homophobic epithet in an off-base assault (just days after his car tires had been slashed on his base). Another found a note tacked to his bunk on the carrier which read, "Leave or Die." And another had a similar threat written in ketchup on his bunk. According to the report, "the ship's command did little to attempt to track down the perpetrators, and instead investigated the private lives of the threatened sailors and questioned their veracity." All of the sailors who complained of harassment were discharged.

In early 1998, the Defense Department released a report showing that the number of people discharged for homosexuality climbed from 850 in 1996 to 997 in 1997.

Defense Secretary William Cohen acknowledged that "some commanders haven't gotten the message" about the administration's policy barring the pursuit and harassment of homosexuals in the military. He ordered new guidelines to explain and enforce it. "I have tried to make it very clear that we want this policy fully and fairly implemented. That means there's to be no pursuit, there's to be no harassment, and if it's taking place, it's something I'm very concerned about," Cohen said. Those who engage in witch hunts, Cohen warned, will themselves "be the subject of their own investigation," and "potentially charged with sexual harassment."

Calling the Navy's attempt to discharge a top enlisted man a "search and destroy mission," a federal judge ordered the reinstatement of the sailor the Navy had dismissed for listing himself as gay on an online computer service.

The ruling came shortly after that same judge temporarily blocked the Navy from dismissing Senior Chief Petty Officer Timothy R. McVeigh, a 17-year Navy veteran, for allegedly violating the military's "don't ask, don't tell" policy on homosexuality.

McVeigh (who has no connection to the convicted Oklahoma City bomber of the same name) was charged with "sodomy and indecent acts" after a civilian woman who works with McVeigh read an America Online (AOL) profile that she believed to be McVeigh's. McVeigh's AOL profile included the word "gay" under a category that asked about marital status.

Critics accused the Navy of invasion of privacy by tracking down the sailor's identity from his AOL profile page in which he called himself merely "Tim."

An AOL employee also violated company policy by providing McVeigh's name in response to an inquiry from an investigator who did not properly identify himself and who did not offer a warrant or court order requiring that the information be turned over. An AOL senior vice president later indicated that the Navy's investigation of McVeigh was not lawful. "[If] the United States government wants personal information about one of our members," said the AOL official, "there's a lawful process and a lawful procedure to follow — it was not followed in this instance."

The federal judge agreed with the Navy's critics, writing, "When the Navy affirmatively took steps to confirm the identity of the e-mail respondent, it violated the very essence of 'Don't Ask, Don't Pursue' by launching a search and destroy mission" against McVeigh.

"[T]his Court ... cannot understand why the Navy would seek to discharge an officer who has serviced his country in a distinguished manner just because he might be gay," wrote the judge.

The judge noted that McVeigh's case "vividly underscores the folly ... of a policy that systematically excludes a whole class of persons who have served this country proudly and in the highest tradition of excellence."

"There is no such thing as a gay person. . . .[homosexuality is] a fictitious identity that is seized on to resolve painful emotional challenges."

Joseph Nicolosi of **National Association for the Research and Therapy of Homosexuality,** at an anti-gay conference in Washington, D.C.

CALIFORNIA

Governor Pete Wilson of **California** characterized as "unnecessary" a bill that would have added sexual orientation to the list of classes protected under the state Fair Employment and Housing Acts (FEHA). The governor returned the bill, unsigned, to the legislature. He had vetoed similar legislation in 1991.

The state Assembly had approved the bill by a 41-38 vote and it passed in the state Senate 22-18. State Senator Dick Mountjoy (R-Monrovia) denounced the bill for giving "special rights" to gays and lesbians and threatened to promote a public referendum to overturn the law if the governor failed to veto the legislation.

During speeches in California, Alveda Celeste King (founder of the conservative "King for America" organization and niece of Dr. Martin Luther King, Jr.) protested that "injustice is being done to family values," complaining that "[t]o equate homosexuality with race is to give a death sentence to civil rights." At a Burbank demonstration sponsored by Concerned Women for America, Alveda King railed, "don't expect us or our children to approve of, promote, or elevate sexual preference to civil rights status... What's next, civil rights on the basis of prostitution and pedophilia?"

James Dobson's *Family News in Focus* radio program expressed fear that if Wilson signed the bill, it would "enshrine homosexual behavior as a protected civil right."

The Capitol Resource Institute (CRI), California's Focus on the Family affiliate, applauded the governor after he returned the bill unsigned, for "protecting the Boy Scouts and public school children from the homosexual agenda." CRI had branded the anti-discrimination legislation as "the crown jewel for the homosexual lobby" and a "virtual Pandora's Box" in press releases and on its website. Michael Bowman, executive director of Capitol Resource Institute, further wrote, "Because of Wilson's veto, private citizens won't be forced to open their homes, schools, businesses, and community organizations to gay activists who want to push their lifestyle on the rest of us."

The University of **California** Board of Regents voted to extend housing and health benefits to the domestic partners of its lesbian and gay employees against the protests and political maneuverings of Governor Pete Wilson (R).

The University of California president was prepared to implement domestic partner benefits on a campus-by-campus basis earlier in the year, but Gov. Wilson used his position on the Board of Regents to place the item before the entire board at a November meeting. Wilson also launched a letter-writing campaign to the University's Regents to defeat the proposal. "It would be unwise and wrong in my judgment for the University of California to create such a far-reaching precedent," wrote Wilson, complaining that the action would be contrary to state policy, erode the institution of marriage and destroy families. Wilson had similarly protested against same-sex employment benefits earlier in the month while speaking before a Christian Coalition meeting in Long Beach, California.

Accused of "stacking the deck," the governor appointed three new Regents supportive of his views, one the day before and two on the very day of the vote. At the meeting, Wilson argued, "The University of California is a public trust and has obligations that private institutions do not have...to uphold the institution of marriage." One Regent agreed, fearing same-sex partner benefits would lead to "a serious moral break-down of Western civilization."

By a close vote of 13 to 12, the full Board of Regents extended spousal benefits to the domestic partners of its lesbian and gay employees — the first statewide agency to do so. Explaining his affirmative vote, Regent Ward Connerly, said "I support the institution of marriage, after 34 years of it. But there are values that transcend marriage: the value of equality, the value of individual liberty, and the value of letting people pursue happiness on their own terms."

At year's end, a California state senator known for his legislative denunciation of same-sex marriage began an equally fervent assault on the newly enacted University of California policy. He introduced SB 1484, which would prohibit any University of California monies allocated by the legislature to be used for domestic partner benefits.

A victim of escalating on-the-job harassment due to his sexual orientation, a **Los Angeles, California** gay man was terminated from Anheuser-Busch in February. The employee had been told by plant management, "To tell co-workers that you are gay is unbecoming to a manager and will result in your termination." The gay man filed suit against the corporation and initiated a nationwide "Boycott Budweiser" campaign.

According to the ex-employee's suit, anti-gay comments began soon after he placed a picture of his significant other on the bulletin board above his desk and was discovered to have recently purchased a home in predominantly gay West Hollywood, characterized by co-workers as "where the faggots live."

According to the lawsuit, a letter from the employee to Anheuser-Busch's Vice President of Human Resources documenting the hostile environment was discounted as false solely at the suggestion of plant management, who offered to investigate the charges themselves. Management rejected the employee's claims without so much as interviewing witnesses because, it alleged, doing so would be too disruptive. Brewery management dismissed the prevalent use of "fag" and "faggot" as mere "shop talk."

According to the gay employee, he was finally terminated for "sexual harassment and sexual misconduct" charges based on allegations made by two co-workers. Under oath, one admitted that his complaint that the fired employee had improperly touched him referred to a time when their shirt sleeves brushed against each other while passing; the other claimed a lewd remark had been made to him. The plant manager also admitted, during pre-trial depositions, to threatening the employee because of his sexual orientation.

After failing to get the case dismissed in Superior Court and the Appellate Court, Anheuser-Busch asked the California Supreme Court to dismiss the complaint, claiming that being gay is a choice and therefore not subject to the jurisdiction of California's civil courts. Anheuser-Busch attorneys withdrew the request for dismissal, however, when the "Boycott Budweiser Coalition" was launched. Gay bars from the west to Wisconsin refused to stock Budweiser and other Anheuser-Busch products.

In December, Anheuser-Busch settled the discrimination suit out of court for an undisclosed sum.

The California State Labor Commissioner ruled in October that **Oakland, California** was in violation of state law by offering medical benefits to same-sex domestic partners.

Oakland offers the same health benefits to domestic partners of its gay and lesbian city employees as it does to heterosexual spouses. The policy came under fire by a male employee unable to obtain medical benefits for his long-term female domestic partner.

The Oakland Deputy City Attorney defended the policy saying it does not discriminate based on sexual orientation but rather provides benefits only to intimate partners who cannot legally marry. The attorney continued, "People with opposite-sex partners are not in the same position. They always have the option to marry." But the labor commissioner said the city provided "no legitimate explanation for offering certain employment benefits to some domestic partners and not others" and ordered Oakland to pay for health insurance for all city employees with registered domestic partners, regardless of sex.

The Air Transport Association (ATA) filed a lawsuit in U. S. District Court in **San Francisco, California** marking one of the most significant challenges to San Francisco's pioneering requirement that all businesses contracting with the city extend the same benefits to unmarried employees' domestic partners that they do to married employees' spouses.

The San Francisco Board of Supervisors passed an ordinance in November 1996 requiring all companies doing business with the city to provide health and other benefits to the domestic partners of their non-married employees if they provide them to married couples. The ordinance, which took effect June 1, 1997, applies to both heterosexual and homosexual couples.

In commenting on the lawsuit, the president and chief executive officer of the ATA stated, "Airlines have always been governed by federal, not local, laws because it would be impossible to operate in hundreds of communities with different and possibly contradictory, local ordinances. A national transportation system requires one regulatory master, and that is the federal government."

The city had given one ATA member, Federal Express, a deadline of February 27 to either comply or forfeit a long-term lease of land at the San

Francisco Airport it had planned to use as a new cargo area. FedEx subsequently filed for and received a court order from a U.S. District Court judge temporarily enjoining the city from renting the land to another tenant.

"It is unfortunate that the city is trying to force an airline to make a decision with regard to such an important legal issue that the courts have not decided," an ATA statement said. Apparently unimpressed, a spokesperson for the San Francisco City Attorney's office replied that, "If they [FedEx] don't like the terms of the lease, they don't have to sign."

A second suit against the ordinance was filed by the American Center for Law and Justice (ACLJ), a legal organization founded by Pat Robertson. That suit contends the ordinance violates both the state and federal constitutions. The San Francisco Catholic Archdiocese also voiced concerns about the law, but the city reached an accord with the Archbishop that allows church employees to designate any member of their household, whether it be an unmarried partner, spouse or relative, to receive benefits.

In November, the San Francisco Board of Supervisors passed an amendment to the ordinance that gave city department heads the power to waive certain ordinance requirements in some cases — with the approval of the city's Human Rights Commission.

Some local gay and lesbian advocates worry that the amendment — however subtle — will ultimately weaken the legislation. "I think it's really important as a principle that the city not water down the legislation, because it's groundbreaking," said one San Francisco community leader.

But the ACLJ sees the ordinance in a different way. The western regional ACLJ counsel called the ordinance "a dagger aimed at the heart of traditional marriage."

"Whenever there is anything new...there is institutional resistance," said one of the three openly gay San Francisco supervisors who authored the ordinance.

And Mayor Willie Brown, an ardent supporter of the ordinance, argued that "[y]ou have separation of church and state. You can't impose the policies of a religious organization on the city government."

Earlier, United Airlines had objected to the provisions of the law, questioning whether companies must offer the benefits nationwide or worldwide, not just in San Francisco. But the airline eventually agreed to comply with the ordinance.

In April 1998, a federal judge ruled in the Air Transport Association lawsuit that San Francisco cannot require airlines to provide health and pension benefits to employees' domestic partners. The judge ruled the ordinance impermissibly created "a regulatory effect on out-of-state activities," but that San Francisco can, under certain circumstances, require airlines to offer benefits that are not regulated by federal law. Those benefits *can* be required for airline employees working in San Francisco and at San Francisco International Airport.

DISTRICT OF COLUMBIA

The federal government's fiscal 1998 appropriations for the **District of Columbia** again included a provision prohibiting the District from using any of its funds to implement a 1992 domestic partners law.

The original Health Care Benefits Expansion Act of 1992 granted health insurance to the partners of District government employees on the condition that partners pay the premium themselves. The 1998 fiscal budget continued a five-year-old federal policy of preventing the District from implementing the law.

"I used the word 'queer' and I'll use it again. I'm not going to call them gay. I don't approve of their lifestyle one bit."

Emory Folmar, Mayor of Montgomery, Alabama, defending his anti-gay remarks on a Montgomery radio program

Rather than wage a hopeless fight against the prohibition, lesbian and gay activists and pro-gay legislators chose instead to support the deferral of amendments to the D.C. appropriations bill on funding domestic benefits until the fiscal 1999 appropriations. Because Congress only continued its "freeze" on funding such benefits rather than repealing the domestic partners law outright, the issue will come up again in 1998.

An anti-gay amendment to the appropriations bill by Rep. Jay Dickey (R-AK) barring unmarried and same-sex couples from adopting children was ruled out of order by the House Rules Committee, so it never reached the House floor for a vote. This was the third year in a row that Dickey has offered the anti-gay amendment. Currently, D.C. law allows same-sex couples to adopt if a court determines they are otherwise qualified and finds the adoption to be in the best interest of the child.

The day of the committee vote, Andrea Sheldon, daughter of the Traditional Values Coalition's (TVC) founder and head, Rev. Lou Sheldon, and TVC's chief lobbyist in Washington, was standing outside the Rules Committee's meeting room urging members to support Dickey's amendment.

FLORIDA

Without public discussion, the **Dade County, Florida** commissioners voted down a measure that would have prohibited discrimination against gay men and lesbians. Moments before the 7-to-5 vote in June, the Metro-Dade County Commission unanimously approved a resolution to "uphold traditional family values."

The defeated amendment would have added sexual orientation to the county's existing anti-discrimination law prohibiting discrimination in employment, housing or lending. A controversial amendment requiring businesses to provide insurance coverage for domestic partners of lesbian and gay employees had been withdrawn.

The local Christian Coalition affiliate distributed fax alerts claiming that the "'special rights for homosexuals' ordinance" would "put your business out of business" by forcing Christian businesses to hire homosexuals and provide health benefits to them and their partners "at a time when Dade County has the second highest AIDS rate in the nation." Another fax alert aimed at churches claimed that the ordinance "would prevent pastors from preaching against the homosexual lifestyle from the pulpit," force them to hire homosexuals to staff daycare centers and Christian private schools and generally "create a hostile environment toward churches who may simply just disagree."

"Where's the evidence of discrimination?" a Christian Coalition lawyer complained. "This is not some powerless group. For them to cry victim is misleading." Another opponent of the ordinance stated, "I don't want my children to be educated by homosexuals."

Members of the Dade County Christian Coalition sang and prayed in the County Commission lobby before and after the vote, carrying signs that read "Be Ashamed of Gay Rights" and "Uphold God's Law." Members spoke in favor of a resolution to uphold "traditional family values" and the audience cheered when the anti-discrimination measure was voted down.

GEORGIA

The U.S. Supreme Court denied a **Georgia** lesbian's appeal and let stand a lower court ruling that the state Attorney General had not acted unlawfully in withdrawing a job offer due to her sexual orientation.

In 1990, then-Georgia Attorney General Michael Bowers made an offer of permanent employment to a summer law intern, Robin Joy Shahar, to work as a staff attorney after she graduated from Emory University. The following year, Bowers withdrew the job offer mere months before Shahar was to start work. Bowers acted after discovering Shahar's July 1991 plans to marry her female partner in a commitment ceremony.

"This action has become necessary in light of information which has only recently come to my attention relating to a purported marriage between you and another woman," Bowers stated in a letter to Shahar. "As chief legal officer of this state, inaction on my part would constitute tacit approval of this purported marriage and jeopardize the proper functioning of this office."

Shahar sued. A 1995 district court ruling recognized Shahar's relationship as a "constitutionally protected intimate association," but concluded that Bowers actions were not unlawful.

In May 1997, the full 11th Circuit U.S. Court of Appeals ruled that Bowers could indeed withdraw Shahar's job offer for participating in a gay marriage ceremony. The court held that it was reasonable to believe that partners in a same-sex union engage in sexual activity in violation of state law.

Shahar asked the court to rehear the case after Bowers — now a candidate for governor — publicly admitted to a ten-year adulterous affair with a woman he once employed. In withdrawing Shahar's job offer, Bowers had expressed concern over public reaction to sexual misconduct in office. Adultery is a misdemeanor crime in Georgia. In August, the appeals court denied Shahar's request by a vote of 9 to 3.

Shahar's request to the U.S. Supreme Court that it hear the case was denied letting stand the lower court ruling that Shahar's rights were not violated when the job offer was withdrawn.

ILLINOIS

A **Cook County, Illinois** circuit court judge approved a Chicago ordinance guaranteeing benefits for same-sex partners of city employees. Opponents attacked the measure as subsidizing "a lifestyle the majority of taxpayers are against."

The legal challenge received financial support from the Focus on the Family-affiliated Illinois Family Institute and the Phoenix-based Alliance Defense Fund. The attorney working on behalf of the conservative Alliance Defense Fund argued that the City Council had exceeded its power when it passed the domestic partner benefits measure in March 1997.

Cook County Circuit Court Judge Thomas Durkin refused to grant a preliminary injunction against the ordinance, stating that the city reserves the authority to make such personnel decisions. Judge Durkin then chastised unnamed letter-writers who had sent him hate-mail saying he would be "condemned to hell" if he did not strike down the measure. "Since it came from professed Christians, I would describe the mail I received as most un-Christian," Judge Durkin lamented, stating that the letter-writers showed "a lack of a basic element — personal charity toward others."

IOWA

A committee of the **Davenport, Iowa** City Council voted unanimously to table a proposed amendment protecting lesbians and gay men from discrimination. The amendment would have added sexual orientation to the city's civil rights ordinance. Proponents said the measure was a reaction to a 1996 incident in which a Davenport nursing home administrator fired six employees because of their perceived sexual orientation, claiming that they lacked appropriate "moral character." The Davenport City Council's Quality Improvement Committee cited a lack of time to study information provided to it by the Davenport Civil Rights Commission as the reason for the six-week postponement.

Prior to the vote, the committee had heard from two opponents of the measure. First, a woman who refused to give her name stated, "As a Christian, I should not be forced to rent to or hire a homosexual." "The issue is about conduct," she said. "I want you to protect society. I want you to protect the children." The host of a local cable-access television show stated his opposition: "The state doesn't recognize gay rights, and neither should we."

The proposed ordinance died in committee. The Human Rights Commission hopes to reintroduce the proposal at some future date.

MARYLAND

The **Harford County, Maryland** Public Library (HCPL) voted to remove "sexual orientation" from the equal opportunity clause of its personnel manual. The library's director explained the removal was "because the clause addressed areas covered by law" and "[s]exual orientation is not protected by law and it is misleading and confusing for it be in the clause."

During a board of trustees meeting, several HCPL staff members voiced "great concern" over the removal. The library's human resources committee also submitted a fair practices statement to the board with sexual orientation added to read: "Appointments, assignments, promotions, terminations and any disciplinary actions shall be made without regard to race, color, religion, sex, age, national origin, marital status, disability, or sexual orientation." Board members declined to add the fair practices statement to the manual, instead preferring an all-inclusive statement that did not single out any minority. The minutes of the meeting stated that one member, in particular, "took exception to putting the fair practices statement in the manual because it singles out certain groups and disregards other groups...including obese people, the white male, etc." Another pointed out that sexual orientation was not a protected class under state civil rights laws.

A **Montgomery County, Maryland** organization of municipal workers and a county government diversity committee endorsed domestic partner benefits for the same-sex partners of county employees shortly after the county's Human Relations Commission rejected a proposal on such benefits.

The Montgomery County Human Relations Commission had voted 6-1 not to endorse domestic partner benefits. Commission members feared the proposal would be viewed as "preferential treatment" for lesbian and gay employees and would "go beyond what is presently being given to county employees." According to a local gay activist working toward passage of the measure, another commissioner said he could not support it on "moral grounds."

Soon after the vote, the Montgomery County Government and Municipal Employees Organization and union negotiators were reported to be insisting upon domestic partner benefits during closed-door contract negotiations. The Diversity Council of Montgomery County — made up of representatives from each department of county government along with additional members from some outside organizations — also officially endorsed domestic partner benefits. In a letter to the county executive and chief administrative officer, the Diversity Council stated it "believes that equality among all employees should be reflected in the benefits package we offer to them."

Local anti-gay crusaders were quick to attack the proposal. "Homosexuality is illegal, immoral, unhealthy and unnatural," said the president of the Woman's Christian Temperance Union. "I don't think any tax money should be going to support domestic partners."

MASSACHUSETTS

Political maneuvering and conservative outrage have shelved a domestic partner benefit ordinance for **Newton, Massachusetts** until 1999.

The domestic partner benefits ordinance was first approved by Newton's Board of Aldermen by a 13-10 vote. The ordinance provided for domestic partner benefits to same-sex and unmarried heterosexual couples. Two alder-men who voted in favor of the policy filed a motion a day later to have the vote reconsidered. One of the aldermen wanted his failed amendment to extend the benefits to "family partners" — blood relatives and others who share financial resources — attached to the ordinance. Three days later the Board voted 18-6 to discard the vote, leaving the city without a domestic partners benefits ordinance. The bill was sent back to committee to reconcile differences through a new "family partners" amendment. Finally, with a compromise reached over the inclusion of blood relatives, the Newton Board of Aldermen passed the ordinance 16-8.

Stand Up Newton, a grassroots organization opposed to the ordinance, vowed to collect the necessary 2,500 signatures needed to get the issue on a city referendum ballot. "This is not only socially radical, but fiscally irresponsible," said the leader of Stand Up Newton. "People are outraged." The group gathered enough signatures over the Christmas and New Year holidays to certify a ballot referendum. However, the local League of Women Voters logged a number of complaints about the deceptive manner in which the opponents collected the signatures.

The Board of Alderman had 30 days from the January 5th petition filing either to schedule the referendum or rescind the measure. The Board of Aldermen voted 14-9 to rescind the "Domestic and Extended Family Partnership Ordinance" and approved a resolution to wait a full year before enacting another ordinance on domestic partnership benefits.

NEW HAMPSHIRE

A labor arbitrator ruled that the University of **New Hampshire** in **Durham** did not violate an anti-discrimination clause in its faculty union contract when it refused to extend domestic partner benefits to a gay employee.

The case began when a university professor attempted to enroll his same-sex partner in the university's health care program in 1994. The university

38   HOSTILE CLIMATE

denied the request, stating that benefit coverage was for married couples, not domestic partners. The employee countered that the university had violated the anti-discrimination clause of the union contract, claiming the health plan's definition of "dependent" discriminated on the basis of sexual orientation and marital status, as state law prohibits same-sex marriages.

The arbitration ruling stated that because the union had never specified during contract negations that the anti-discrimination clause would apply to the extension of health benefits to domestic partners, the University of New Hampshire board was justified in assuming it had no obligation to extend benefits to the same-sex partners of its lesbian and gay employees. The arbitrator stressed her ruling was strictly concerned with a contractual agreement and was "not a question of whether domestic partner health coverage is wise or unwise, warranted or unwarranted."

The university professor who chairs the union's grievance committee felt the decision was discriminatory. "We seem to have a strange double standard that if you're heterosexual and you're allowed to get married, your partner gets benefits. But if you're homosexual and are not allowed to marry, your partner does not get benefits," she stated. "The whole purpose of providing benefits is to recruit the best people that you can. And this is a *de facto* way of saying that gays and lesbians are not the best people we can get."

The *Manchester Union Leader* had editorialized, "The state should decline to embrace a policy that would further weaken the already shaky institution of the family."

The chairman of the board's personnel committee noted that his committee would again address the issue of domestic benefits. Many university trustees expressed fears that offering health benefits for same-sex partners would upset conservative state legislators and possibly threaten future state funding for the university. The personnel committee chair stated, "For us to deny in any way that there is a political side to this would be folly. But I would hope that whatever vote was taken would be an honest vote based on people's perception about what is really right to do, not what is politically correct to do in a conservative state. It's going to be a hard sell."

NEW YORK

The State University of **New York** at **New Paltz** suspended its search for a dean after members of the community complained about one of its three finalists, a lesbian ex-nun. Critics charged the women was also a witch. The candidate admitted she did participate in ritual circles celebrating solstices, equinoxes and full moons and liked to call herself a witch "because the word carries such a patriarchal taboo." Critics pointed to a passage in her book on lesbian nuns, where she stated "a solidarity with the women who were burned as witches."

An opponent from the National Catholic Forum circulated inflammatory press releases sensationalizing, "Satanism, Sorcery, Drug Use, Sexual Orgies:

The College at New Paltz's Future?" The long-time SUNY critic also complained, "It becomes an alarming community matter to see a self-professed witch being courted by members of the New Paltz faculty and may well assume control over one of SUNY New Paltz's most important academic departments."

Critics of the candidate enlisted a local Republican politician into the fray. "The controversy here is that [the woman] has expanded her personal lifestyle of witchcraft, pagan rituals, lesbianism and lesbianism in the convent into a rather narrow 'academic' focus," the assemblyman said. "I hope that the university will agree that other candidates would provide a more universal perspective on the liberal arts and that [she] is clearly not the best candidate."

SUNY New Paltz suspended its search for a College of Liberal Arts and Sciences dean in May. As this report went to press, the position was still listed as vacant.

NORTH CAROLINA

A **Mitchell County, North Carolina** sheriff ordered the illegal taping of phone conversations that led to the resignation of the local high school football coach, a gay man.

Beginning in 1995, the sheriff had ordered his deputies to tape private phone conversations they picked up over their police scanner. He then threatened to make tapes of the "closeted" coach's phone conversations public unless high school officials fired the gay man. The coach resigned. The incident came to light when one of the deputies involved applied for a job elsewhere and noted that he may have broken the law by taping the conversations. The Mitchell County district attorney then petitioned the courts to have the sheriff removed from office for violating state law prohibiting the interception of private telephone calls.

During the court hearing, the sheriff and county officials reached an agreement that allowed the sheriff to keep his job, but required that he make a public apology and forfeit two weeks of salary. The sheriff announced that although he held "strong personal feelings that persons who follow certain lifestyles should not be employed in particular areas of the public school system, I realize that every citizen is entitled to recognition of his privacy."

The State Bureau of Investigation is also looking into charges against the sheriff. Federal law makes it illegal for a third party to record phone conversations without consent of at least one of the parties involved or a judge's order.

PENNSYLVANIA

Attempts by **Philadelphia, Pennsylvania** to provide domestic partner benefits to same-sex partners of city employees ran into opposition from both a conservative city council president and the city's religious leaders.

The city council president — who opposed granting benefits to same-sex partners on moral and fiscal grounds — obtained a temporary restraining order in June blocking a mayoral order granting domestic partner benefits. The council president sought to prove the measure violated the city's Fair Practices Act.

In November, a trio of councilmen introduced three domestic partnership measures: one, amending city-funded retirement funds so employees could name benefit designees other than blood relatives or a spouse; second, broadening the city real estate tax exemptions to include same-sex couples; and a third, amending the Fair Practices Act to include protection for "life partners," defined as a person of the same sex who shares a residence, income and their resources with someone who is not related by blood and who is in a committed relationship. Each of the measures had 11 co-sponsors among the 17 council members. A council majority also petitioned the council president to hold hearings on the three measures.

The Archdiocese of Philadelphia immediately voiced its strong opposition to domestic partner benefits: "We remain opposed and disappointed that this issue continues to be revisited despite our well-known opposition." The archdiocese asked Catholic parishioners to call and write their council members and said it would "remind our constituents how their council members voted on these issues."

The Cardinal of the Archdiocese wrote the city council expressing his "strong opposition" to the three ordinances: "Ordinances of this type are destructive to our city's moral and social structure because they are, in essence, a means to promote and protect homosexual relations." A local Religious Right group also worked with Muslims, Orthodox Jews and "a vast host of black, Hispanic and Asian clergy who are opposed to expanding the definition of family."

A proponent on the council said the legislation is about fairness, not morality. "We're supposed to treat all citizens equally...so no citizen is left out or discriminated against because of the relationships they're in," he said.

The city council passed all three bills in May 1998. The conservative Urban Family Council announced it would form a PAC to unseat those city council members who voted for the domestic partner benefits package.

A **Pittsburgh, Pennsylvania** gay police officer filed a lawsuit against the city for denying health benefits to same-sex partners of city employees. When the officer designated a same-sex partner as a beneficiary in the city's health benefits program, the application was returned with a letter of rejection. Pittsburgh provides health benefits to the spouses of its heterosexual employees.

The officer's attorney filed a complaint with the Pittsburgh Human Relations Commission. She said, "They flat out told this officer, 'you don't fit the definition in our agreement for dependents.'" Marriage, she argued, is an unrealistic criterion to determine benefits. "Gay people can never meet that definition," she said. The attorney claims that by denying benefits to same-sex partners, the city violated its own 1990 law making it illegal to discriminate on the basis of sexual orientation in matters of employment, housing or public accommodation.

SOUTH CAROLINA

Republican Party officials in **Charleston County, South Carolina** demanded an investigation of a party official, a gay state prosecutor. Officials accused the prosecutor of using his office computer for viewing pornographic pictures and soliciting sex over the Internet. The gay man denied using state money or equipment to download pornography or solicit sex. "I have done nothing illegal," he said.

"I have always felt matters of a personal nature are private and not something anyone, politician or otherwise, need to be judged exclusively on," the prosecutor explained. "It's the performance of the job that counts." Although Republican Party officials deny the man's homosexuality was a motive in their decision, a county executive committeeman said the prosecutor's sexual orientation was indeed a factor in calling for the investigation.

Not all Republicans supported the investigation. One of the state party's matriarchs said, "He has been doing his job, and he has not been offensive in any way with his lifestyle. He hasn't tried to force the way he feels about it on other people, and I don't see any reason for them to force the way they feel about it on him."

The state attorney general's office is investigating the charges. State policy says employees can be disciplined if they use state-owned computers for "immoral purposes."

UTAH

An 18-year-veteran tenured high school teacher in **Spanish Fork, Utah**, was fired as volleyball coach at Spanish Fork High School. She was also told by her principal that "perception" of her had changed and warned that she would lose her job teaching physical education and psychology. The school district issued a highly restrictive "gag" order prohibiting her from speaking about her sexual orientation. In addition, the teacher was excommunicated from the Mormon Church and was sued by a parents' group for allegedly requiring students to disclose dreams they had, for administering personality tests to her students, contributing to the delinquency of minors and for failing to follow state mandates for teachers regarding being a role model.

Wendy Weaver was the target of all this action simply because, in an off-hours telephone inquiry, she acknowledged to a student that she was a lesbian. "In all my years of service to the school district, I've never done anything to deserve this," said Weaver. "I'm not ashamed of my sexuality and I believe they are discriminating against me because of that."

Weaver filed a lawsuit in federal court seeking to end the Nebo School District's severe restrictions on her freedom to discuss her sexual orientation. The district had earlier sent Weaver a written threat of termination should she "make comments, announcements or statements to students, staff members or parents regarding [her] homosexual orientation or lifestyle." The warning continued, "If students, staff members or parents of students ask about your sexual orientation or anything concerning the subject, you shall tell them that the subject is private and personal and inappropriate to discuss with them."

The American Civil Liberties Union (ACLU) has joined the case, arguing that the district's gag order amounts to an unconstitutional violation of free expression, personal privacy and equal protection.

"It's [the gag order] really so extreme that it means she can't talk to anyone," remarked Weaver's attorney. And one self-described "volleyball mom" labeled the whole ordeal a "witch hunt."

A trustee of the Nebo Citizens for Moral and Legal Values countered, "We are not on a witch hunt, but when she went public, it changed the whole outlook."

"When a teacher chooses to openly rebel against the teachings of the Bible, the way Wendy Weaver has, it is not possible for them to be models of moral virtue," according to the American Family Association's *AFA Alert*.

"I've been a good coach and a good teacher. I've never done anything that has infringed on anybody," said Weaver. "Then all of a sudden, I was not living the lifestyle they wanted me to live or being the role model I had always been." Weaver's volleyball teams have won four state championships and she was named 1994 Honors Coach of the Year.

"It would not matter if Wendy Weaver had won coach of the year every year in the past decade," wrote *AFA Alert's* editor, "if her actions teach our children that the commandments of God are something to be ignored." The attorney for the Spanish Fork High School parents and other county residents commented, "Ms. Weaver may win her federal lawsuit," said the attorney, "but a different result will ensue under those [state] laws that were divinely inspired and that I believe will be divinely enforced."

Said one Spanish Folk High parent: "I don't think we have anything to be ashamed of, simply because we may not be as open-minded as some people want us to be."

VIRGINIA

The **Virginia** attorney general issued an opinion declaring that the **Arlington County** policy to extend health insurance to the unmarried — homosexual and heterosexual — partners of county employees is illegal.

The attorney general opined that the policy violated Virginia law, as Arlington County did not get specific permission from the state legislature to extend health insurance to the unmarried partners and other adult dependents of county employees. Virginia law bars local governments from enacting legislation that exceeds the mandates of the state legislature. The county's original request to the state legislature never made it out of committee; the county then determined that the fact that it self insures allows it to set insurance policy without consulting the legislature. The domestic partner benefits policy was unanimously passed by the five-member county board in April.

A conservative state delegate from another county who sought the opinion from the attorney general claimed that the decision will help enforce the state's ban on sodomy: "One of the big problems of this is you're granting a benefit to an employee that's predicated on a violation of state criminal law. That's just not sound public policy."

An Arlington County board member called the opinion part of a "pattern of abuse" against human rights. "This is the right-wing Christian Coalition head of the [governor's] administration raising itself once again," he said.

A few months after the attorney general's opinion, three Arlington County residents filed a lawsuit challenging the county policy. They are represented by Jordan Lorence, a right-wing attorney formerly on the staff of Concerned Women for America.

The **Charlottesville, Virginia** school board rejected an anti-discrimination provision protecting gay and lesbian faculty. The board had been approached by a parent who is also an adult advisor for a gay and lesbian youth church group. His proposal was in response to the near-fatal beating of a Charlottesville gay man by two teenagers and an adult.

"Unfortunately, none of the school divisions in the Charlottesville area explicitly ban discrimination [on] the basis of sexual orientation," he said. "Thus, the local situation is one of official indifference."

The Charlottesville school board voted 6-1 to approve a new personnel policy manual *without* a provision prohibiting discrimination based on sexual orientation. The superintendent said that while he "would not discriminate on any basis other than performance," the school board should not add "more due process rights for employees than the law requires." An attorney for the school board said that adding more protections than required by state or federal employment law could lead to frivolous and expensive lawsuits.

WASHINGTON

By a 60 - 40 percent vote, **Washington** state voters defeated a November ballot initiative that would have banned job discrimination based on sexual orientation.

Gay political leaders blamed the defeat on the fact that the National Rifle Association turned out a conservative voting bloc to defeat a gun control initiative also on the ballot and those voters voted no on Initiative 677, the anti-discrimination measure. "The primary issue was the NRA coming in and spending [millions] on educating the people to say 'no' on initiative 676, a pro-gun control initiative," said an attorney and citizen sponsor of the pro-gay initiative.

"The NRA sent in their A-team, headed by Charlton Heston, to make sure they didn't lose a foothold in the state, and in the last two weeks of the campaign, they spent $3 million on advertising to make sure people voted no," said an openly gay Seattle City Council member. As a result, she added, many conservative voters who don't typically participate in off-year elections participated in the November 4th election.

Passage of the initiative would have made Washington the first state to ban job discrimination against gays and lesbians through a voter referendum.

An anti-677 coalition called NOPE — No Official Preferential Employment — enlisted the assistance of both the state and national offices of the Christian Coalition.

"People who want to advance a homosexual agenda have run up against t he public saying this is enough," said the head of the Christian Coalition of Washington. "I do not think there is a climate in America for creating special classes for anyone at all." The Christian Coalition's national office distributed 250,000 voter guides through churches.

 NOPE also managed to obtain the very public support of former Seattle Seahawks football star Steve Largent, now a U. S. Representative from Oklahoma, in a full-page newspaper advertisement.

The Washington State Bar Association, the state's League of Women Voters, the Washington Education Association, and the Washington Association of Churches endorsed the pro-gay measure. Additionally, Governor Gary Locke and progressive African Americans, including clergy, spoke in favor of the initiative.

Opposition to the initiative, however, was loud, ugly and often inaccurate.

"They still want your kids," said a NOPE fundraising letter, "and Initiative 677 is another move toward that goal." The head of NOPE also claimed that gay people are rich and powerful and do not experience discrimination.

The director of a Seattle-based anti-gay organization also suggested that "[g]ranting homosexuals minority status is a serious problem not just for small businesses but for Christians too. You see, if the homosexual community is given minority status they will be protected under our constitution as minorities." He also claimed that Initiative 677 would force fundamentalist

Christian organizations to hire homosexuals or face lawsuits. However, Initiative 677 explicitly exempted religious organizations.

WISCONSIN

The **Milwaukee, Wisconsin** city council rejected a proposal to extend health and funeral leave benefits to unmarried — homosexual or heterosexual — partners of city employees.

The initial version of the ordinance pertained only to the gay and lesbian partners of city employees. The city attorney's office issued an opinion that the proposal must also include heterosexual partners or it would violate the state's Fair Employment Act by discriminating on the basis of sexual orientation. The sponsoring alderman added heterosexual partners to the proposal.

Prior to a Finance and Personnel Committee meeting on the proposal, opponents gathered outside city hall protesting "gay sex" and "sodomites and fornicators." Critics also wore small placards declaring "No taxation for perversion!" during the meeting.

A woman argued the proposal "would run roughshod over deeply held moral convictions" and was a "first step toward endorsing moral anarchy."

The city council voted 14-3 against the proposed ordinance. Two aldermen who voted against the proposal expressed financial concerns.

CULTURE WARS

As more and more positive images of lesbians and gay men appear on our television and movie screens, anti-gay forces have stepped up their efforts to censor them. The Right uses boycotts of sponsors and producers, and continues to fight for repeal of public funding for the arts, the ultimate goal being the elimination of all positive portrayals — and an accompanying increase in the negative portrayals — of lesbian and gay lives.

The Southern Baptist Convention voted in June to boycott the Walt Disney Company and urged the 15.6 million members of the Convention to each withhold at least $100 a year they might have otherwise spent on Disney theme parks, movies, or merchandise. The Convention voted to boycott because of their belief that Disney had moved away from "enriching family entertainment" and toward an increase in anti-Christian bigotry, sexually explicit and violent movies, and support of homosexuality through same-sex benefits for Disney employees.

The American Family Association (AFA) and Catholic League for Religious and Civil Rights have long been sponsoring their own boycotts of Disney for films such as *Priest* and also for Disney's failure to block the annual unofficial Gay Day event at Walt Disney World, same-sex benefits for Disney employees, and Disney-owned ABC's "Ellen" coming "out of the closet in the super bowl of lesbianism."

Praising the Baptists' move but stopping short of endorsing their boycott, Christian Coalition executive director Randy Tate explained, "We have traditionally not engaged in boycotts." Yet, following a news report on the fall television season (Disney/ABC carries two shows — "Nothing Sacred" and "Ellen" — that particularly offended boycotters), Pat Robertson told "700 Club" viewers, "They're pushing the envelope, and Disney, which was known as the family organization, is becoming the family of homosexuality and anti-religious bigotry." Robertson challenged his audience, "If you want to get them, get them in their pocketbooks...tell everybody who advertises on a program like this that you intend to boycott their products."

James Dobson jumped on the boycott bandwagon in May, urging millions of Focus on the Family radio listeners to join the boycott.

Concerned Women for America (CWA) joined after its demands "that [Disney] would stop promoting a pro-homosexual, anti-Christian agenda" were not met during a meeting with Disney officials.

Other organizations joining the "struggle to defend morality and decency in the culture" included: Free Will Baptists, Southern Methodist Church,

> *"What some of our corporate leaders and many other Americans fail to understand, including you, is that tolerance is good when defined to oppose racial, gender, ethnic and/or religious bigotry. However, when tolerance is expanded to include the acceptance of sexually deviant behavior, including the seducing of naive adults and children and the abandonment of moral standards, it is time to become intolerant...."*
>
> County commissioner in Mecklenburg County, North Carolina, objecting to a fellow commissioner's support for an openly gay political candidate

Presbyterian Church in America, Dr. D. James Kennedy and Coral Ridge Ministries, the Christian Family Network (CFN), The Christian Civic League of Maine, Alveda King and King for America, Catholics United for the Faith, conservative commentator Alan Keyes, The Catholic League, General Council of the Assemblies of God (USA), Church of God, the Church of the Nazarene, the International Church of the Foursquare Gospel, the Association of Independent Methodists, Oklahoma State Church of God, *Texas Catholic* (news journal of the Catholic Diocese of Dallas) and *Charisma* magazine (a charismatic movement periodical).

In November, the Southern Baptist Convention mailed fliers to more than 90,000 pastors urging them to encourage their congregations to write to Disney Chairman Michael Eisner and pledge support for the boycott.

The Walt Disney Company reported record revenues of $22.5 billion in 1997.

The personal and on-air 'coming out' of comedian Ellen DeGeneres and her television character "Ellen" caused an uproar among the Religious Right.

The right-wing Media Research Center ran a full page advertisement in *Variety* denouncing the program as a "blatant attempt by Disney, ABC and 'Ellen' to promote homosexuality to America's families." Pat Robertson (Christian Coalition), Phyllis Schlafly (Eagle Forum) and Jerry Falwell were among those Religious Right leaders who signed the 'open letter' condemning the episode as a "slap in the face to America's families."

Robert Knight (Family Research Council) warned that the comedy was "part of a larger agenda to saturate prime-time television with homosexual-affirmative themes."

The American Family Association (AFA) and Christian Family Network (CFN) responded with an e-mail and letter campaign to advertising sponsors. Tipped off by an intercepted pro-gay listener's e-mail, AFA and CFN called on their online members to respond to an ABC News online poll asking, "Would you allow your child to watch a lesbian kiss on television?" The poll was a response to Ellen DeGeneres's same-sex kiss on an episode of "Ellen." The CFN alert chastised ABC on grounds that "entertainment's function is not to re-program our children with the homosexual agenda of normalization." The group requested that "family members nationwide give their input. After all, we are the ones who have the children!!" Buoyed by four separate right-wing 'action alerts,' the final straw poll narrowly favored saying "no" to allowing children to watch a lesbian kiss on television.

AFA also protested the planned appearance by DeGeneres on the Public Broadcasting System's "Sesame Street" and "Storytime" programs for children, claiming that the "Hollywood-New York-Washington, D.C. axis has strategically chosen the next generation as their safest bet for normalizing" homosexuality and urging members to complain to Congress about "tax money being used to convince our children and grandchildren that there is nothing wrong with being gay."

The Christian Family Network and AFA continued a near-weekly barrage of alerts on "Ellen," chastising Disney/ABC for "constant promotion of the homosexual agenda" and "toxic media poison." CFN rallied its membership against the company's "agenda-driven programming" of DeGeneres's "weekly soapbox to change public perception."

By year's end, some ABC affiliates complained that the show's content had driven away local advertisers, particularly those in the south. CFN deduced that "["Ellen"] has done nothing but force the homosexual line on the public and the public wants no part in the normalization of this abhorrent lifestyle....advertisers do not want to be associated with this type of program which is unfriendly to family values."

In April 1998 — nearly one year after its ground-breaking "coming out" episode — "Ellen" was cancelled by ABC television for low ratings. The Christian Family Network claimed the ratings drop "reflect[ed] the sentiment of mainstream America" who "want[ed] no part in the normalization of this abhorrent lifestyle."

The Universal Press-syndicated comic strip *For Better or For Worse* was censored from at least 30 daily newspapers for a series of cartoons dealing with the romantic concerns of a gay teenage character. Additionally, three newspapers canceled the strip altogether. Universal Press had sent editors advance notice of the upcoming gay-themed series. Papers in Ohio, Texas, Kansas and Alabama were among those that chose not to run the gay-themed panels during September. *For Better or For Worse* runs in about 1,700 newspapers.

Cartoonist Lyn Johnston had first come under fire for introducing Lawrence, a gay teen, to the popular cartoon in 1993. At least 17 papers had canceled the strip when the gay character was first introduced; another 50 requested rerun strips. The new controversy focused on a story line in which Lawrence's boyfriend chooses to move to Paris to study piano.

The Christian Family Network (CFN) condemned the series for its "homo-sympathetic" portrayal of gay relationships and a "blatant disregard for values and morality." CFN president Don Jackson lamented, "The comic page...is one place in the newspaper that should be safe from unhealthy agendas. Cartoonists and newspapers have a responsibility to ensure that the comic page is available for safe, healthy, enjoyable entertainment. This page should not be used as an indoctrination tool for the homosexual lifestyle...homosexuality is immoral, unscriptural and unhealthy."

CFN urged its members who were subscribers to those newspapers carrying *For Better or For Worse* to request that their papers not be delivered on the days the gay-themed story line was published. Jackson warned editors, "[T]his is not a boycott of newspapers, but is a way of letting all involved know that the American public is unwilling to be an accomplice to the liberal homosexual agenda."

The American Family Association (AFA) forwarded CFN's press release to its own electronic mailing list, asking AFA members to join in the action of canceling subscriptions for those days the controversial strips were carried.

The Religious Right continued throughout the year to attack the National Endowment for the Arts (NEA) for funding "homosexual propaganda."

Gary Bauer, president of the Family Research Council (FRC), stated in a fundraising letter: "We must end funding for the homosexual propaganda spread through the National Endowment for the Arts and through AIDS programs that misspend our tax dollars." FRC urged its members to contact Congress and demand that they defund the agency. In its *Current Issues of Concern*, Focus on the Family described *It's Elementary: Teaching About Gay Issues in School* — partially supported by NEA funds to the Northwest Film Center — as "a so-called educational film that is a brazen attempt to promote homosexuality to America's schoolchildren and equates Christians with Nazis."

The same Focus on the Family action alert branded the videos by another NEA recipient, Women Make Movies, a 25-year old distributor of women's films, as full of "incest, sado-masochism, lesbianism, child pornography and pedophilia." Women Make Movies called the claims unfair; the American Family Association (AFA) had circulated to members of Congress out-of-context excerpts from their films about lesbian sexuality and women's reproductive health practices, labeling them "hard core pornography." Women Make Movies also helped to produce the controversial *The Watermelon Woman*. Rep. Peter Hoekstra (R-MI) accused the film distributors of using taxpayer money from the NEA "to fund production and distribution of patently offensive and possibly pornographic films."

FRC's Gary Bauer also led a coalition of Religious Right leaders asking Congress to stand by its promise to defund the NEA. Members of the Family Research Council-led coalition included: Empower America (William Bennett and Jack Kemp), Christian Action Network (Martin Mawyer), Christian Coalition, Concerned Women for America (Carmen Pate), American Family Association, Americans for Tax Reform (Grover Norquist), Eagle Forum, Traditional Values Coalition (Rev. Louis Sheldon) and conservative movie critic/radio host Michael Medved.

In response to pro-"Ellen" statements by Vice President Al Gore, Christian Coalition executive director Randy Tate slammed Gore as "so far to the left he's left America" by "giving legitimacy to a lifestyle that centers around actions that the majority of Americans view as morally wrong." Tate complained on his organization's website that Gore's remarks gave "alternative lifestyle choices such as homosexuality a veneer of legitimacy." Further statements from former Vice President Dan Quayle, conservative commentator Alan Keyes, Rep. J.C. Watts, Jr. (R-OK) and the Family Research

Council (FRC) challenged Gore's praise of the comedy's openly lesbian character. Robert Knight (FRC) declared "Vice President Al Gore's remarks concerning 'Ellen' have tipped the hand of the administration's pro-homosexual agenda."

A gospel duo targeted gay men and lesbians in one of its songs, and gained a great deal of notoriety by doing so. "It's Not Natural" by Angie and Debbie Winans was written in response to Ellen DeGeneres's television character "coming out" in "Ellen." The song, from the sisters' Bold album, criticizes unwed mothers, pornography and homosexuality. The record appears on a label formed by Angie's husband and brother-in-law "to uphold Godly standards in this business." Angie and Debbie Winans are the two youngest sisters in the popular gospel family.

"The gay lifestyle is promoted in our entertainment world. When you watch TV or listen to music or movies, those things are glorified and in time accepted as the way it should be," Debbie Winans said. "We are just trying to put an alternative perspective out there."

Fanning the controversy and sales, the Washington, D.C.-based promoters of the album sent a press release to the local gay newspaper, announcing that the song "is igniting controversy in Gay communities, including Gay churches, because it denounces homosexuality and attacks the Gay movement."

The executive director of the National Black Lesbian and Gay Leadership Forum (NBLGLF) took exception to the young Winans' message: "They're using the Gospel to divide people, especially black people, who've been divided already. The very same Bible they attempt to quote to justify their homophobia has been used against blacks to justify racism."

The Gay & Lesbian Alliance Against Defamation (GLAAD) attempted to arrange a meeting between the duo and leadership from the black and religious communities supportive of gay men and lesbians. A scheduled meeting was canceled by the Winans, but the sisters did appear on a BET (Black Entertainment Television) forum to discuss the song with ministers on both sides of the issue and the NBLGLF executive director.

While lesbians, gay men and their supporters boycotted appearances by the sisters and asked radio stations not to play the offending song, Lifeline — a long-distance company promoted by many right-wing groups — offered complimentary copies of the "It's Not Natural" music video to youth because of its "positive message."

Angie and Debbie Winans have since lobbied Congress on behalf of the anti-gay Traditional Values Coalition, urging legislators to reject the Employment Non-Discrimination Act (ENDA), proposed federal employment protection for lesbians and gays.

ALASKA

In **Anchorage, Alaska** the state Christian Coalition affiliate campaigned against Out North Theater, host to many programs dealing with gay issues. The Christian Coalition of Alaska had raised objections over public funding of Out North's education programs, noting that concerned parents were "uncomfortable with members of a gay, alternative theater group approaching and building relationships with children who are vulnerable."

Finally, in mid-November, the Anchorage Assembly voted 6-5 to curtail city funding for Out North. Said assembly member Ted Carlson, "We don't want to use tax money to pay for something that the whole family can't go to."

The openly gay managers of Out North were also involved in a lawsuit challenging the state's ban on same-sex marriages and they expressed the belief that the city's actions against the theater were punishment for their activism.

ALABAMA

A sole ABC affiliate — WBMA in **Birmingham, Alabama** — refused to air the "coming out" episode of the comedy "Ellen." Officials at the station claimed the April 30th episode was not appropriate "family viewing."

Lesbian and gay activists in the community, however, saw the decision to drop the episode as a form of censorship. "This is a black eye for Birmingham. The people of Alabama are fully capable of making their own decision about whether or not to tune into this episode," a spokesperson for the Gay and Lesbian Alliance of Alabama stated.

Spurred on by the American Family Association, calls and letters to the station ran 2-to-1 in favor of blocking the broadcast. WBMA-TV 33/40 blacked out the episode itself, the follow-up "Prime Time Live" interview with Ellen DeGeneres, and "Entertainment Tonight." WBMA also refused to air subsequent episodes in which Ellen DeGeneres's character told friends and family she was gay.

Attempts by local and national gay rights groups to secure an alternate location for a satellite broadcast of the program ran up against fears of the event being "way too controversial." Finally, a Birmingham auditorium was procured for a "Welcome Out 'Ellen' Party" broadcast, and it was the largest gay, lesbian, bisexual and transgender event in Alabama history, with a crowd estimated at over 2,500.

The affiliate finally agreed to air an August rerun of the original episode.

CALIFORNIA

Two women held a gay-themed book from the **Belmont, California** public library hostage. One, a parent, criticized the text and illustrations of *The New Joy of Gay Sex* for being too graphic and inappropriate for a public library collection visited by children. She said that the manual "doesn't meet the standards set forth by society" and first asked that the book be moved to a special adult section. The library denied her request.

Failing to get the sole copy of the book pulled from general circulation, the two women then demanded that the title be removed from the library. The mother then arranged for her friend to check the book out and kept it in a storage locker. Both women claimed that the request to remove the book had nothing to do with homosexuality, although neither objected to its heterosexual counterpart, *The New Joy of Sex*.

The San Mateo County Librarian appointed a three-librarian panel to investigate the request for removal. The panel voted in September to retain *The New Joy of Gay Sex* in general circulation, stating, "While we acknowledge that the book's contents may offend some, we believe that it is a useful and singular resource for its intended audience."

The overdue book was not returned by the protesters. Several copies of *The New Joy of Gay Sex* were donated to the Belmont library to replace the missing volume.

An art gallery in **San Francisco, California** was repeatedly vandalized during an exhibition of artworks depicting same-sex affection. On two separate occasions, rocks and a wooden traffic barrier were thrown through the windows of Galeria de la Raza located in the city's Mission District. Two artworks were destroyed in the attacks. The controversial artworks depicted homosexual kissing between religious figures, Latino community heroes and pop icons, such as portraits of Madonna kissing Mother Theresa and Che Guevara embracing Cesar Chavez. The exhibit's purpose was to "investigate issues such as gender identities, queer sexuality, cultural fantasy and the nature of our religious structures."

> *"Homosexuality is illegal, immoral, unhealthy and unnatural. . . .I don't think any tax money should be going to support domestic partners."*
>
> President of the **Women's Christian Temperance Union**, opposing Montgomery County, Maryland's proposed policy to provide domestic partnership benefits to county employees

Gallery officials held a community forum on the controversial exhibition. More than 200 people attended the forum; many supported the gallery, while others were critical of the owners for not anticipating the community response. A gallery volunteer said, "There is a big difference between provoking thought and provoking violence."

A photorealist painting celebrating the 1993 National March on Washington For Lesbian, Gay and Bi-Equal Rights was defaced while displayed at a downtown **San Francisco, California** gallery.

Frank Pietronigro's *Kelvin's Majesty* was vandalized with a scrawled expletive during a retrospective exhibit at The Lurie Company's Atrium Gallery. "The nature of this painting was irrevocably altered by this hateful incident," stated the artist. "[T]his painting...was created to celebrate lesbian and gay pride."

The painting was removed for the remainder of the exhibit.

FLORIDA

Anti-gay protesters picketed outside Disney World in **Lake Buena Vista, Florida** and created a two-mile traffic backup when they moved their demonstration into neighboring **Kissimmee.**

The anti-choice group Operation Rescue, which is expanding its mission to include opposition to homosexuality, targeted Disney for providing health benefits to partners of its lesbian and gay employees, promoting an annual "Gay Day" in Orlando, and the "anti-Christian, pro-homosexual themes" in some of its movies and television shows. Four-foot-by-four-foot placards blared "Disney Promotes Homosexuality" and "If you love Jesus, turn around." The group handed out American Family Association leaflets listing reasons why people should boycott the Walt Disney Company.

The Rev. Flip Benham, leader of the Texas-based Operation Rescue, denounced "[t]he once family-friendly Disney" for becoming "a platform through which the radical homosexual agenda" is being forced on American children.

Three protesters — including Benham — were fined for obstruction of a public street and throwing or placing advertising material on a moving vehicle. The arrests occurred after police warned the protesters about walking into a major intersection. The 75 to 100 people involved in the protests included representatives of ten churches and also high school students attending an Operation Rescue conference nearby. Operation Rescue called the post-holiday December action the first in a year-long "massive attack on the gates of hell" at what it calls the "Tragic Kingdom."

MASSACHUSETTS

Public outrage centered around a sexually explicit photograph, part of an exhibit with "very strong gay content" displayed at a **Provincetown, Massachusetts** art museum. The photograph displayed at the Provincetown Art Association and Museum (PAAM) depicted a nude man holding his erect penis. Local residents and artisans complained about the image, some labeling the male nude as "pornography, plain and simple."

Two exhibiting artists removed their works from secondary galleries at PAAM to protest the controversial photograph's prominent placement in the museum's front gallery. They complained about the public location of "A Strong Breed: Emerging Artists Show, 1997" — which included several male nudes and couplings of nude women — in the entry area where young children could easily view the images.

One artist, who removed her paintings and who was also a PAAM Board of Trustees member, requested that a notice alerting patrons to the sexually-charged nature of the exhibition be posted. She accused the show's curator and artists of being ACT-UP members (a charge she later recanted) pushing an extreme agenda. She complained to the local press: "I felt there was a definite, maybe unconscious, bias against family in the show."

An enraged letter to the newspaper about "these so-called 'alternative lifestyle' artists" charged, "These ACT-UP queers try to push their views on us in the name of First Amendment rights and the curators of the museum go right along with it."

The photograph was purchased from the show by a local gay businessman.

NORTH CAROLINA

A **North Carolina** general assembly amendment to restrict objectionable content in taxpayer-funded art exhibits or performances was dropped in budget negotiations. A similar provision appeared in last year's budget but it expired when the state's fiscal year ended June 30, 1997. The current amendment would have written the measure permanently into law.

Arts advocacy proponents and gay rights activists in North Carolina have become increasingly entangled in local battles over the homosexual content in theatrical performances funded in part by public money.

"If you have any respect for the representative system of governance, then the idea of spending these dollars on something a small minority supports is offensive," the Republican sponsor of the failed amendment said. "My amendment was not censorship; it was allowing the majority of the people the voters elected to make a decision based on the community's standards."

Free speech advocates labeled the amendment "mean-spirited" and restrictive.

Gay and lesbian students at the University of **North Carolina, Chapel Hill** withdrew their scheduled interactive art exhibit when a student activities board imposed last-minute restrictions.

Bisexuals, Gays, Lesbians and Allies for Diversity (B-GLAD), a campus group, designed the "Define Queer" exhibit with wall space around each artwork, encouraging viewers to record their opinions about homosexuality around the art.

Hours before the opening of "Define Queer," the co-chair of the Carolina Union Activities Board demanded that the group shield the public comments by either displaying them in an enclosed booth or having viewers write their comments down in a book instead of directly on the wall around each artwork.

B-GLAD canceled the exhibit, explaining the restrictions would have defeated the art show's defined purpose of creating an open forum for discussion.

A gay activist group based in **Edneyville, North Carolina** filed suit against the publishers and owners of the Raleigh *News & Observer* for libel and defamation.

The Hollywood Reporter, an entertainment trade publication, reported in July that the North Carolina-based Citizens Against Discrimination (CAD) had called for a film industry boycott of the state. CAD said the suggested boycott was to protest anti-gay sentiment in the state, later citing events such as the Mecklenburg County Commission's cut in arts funding over *Angels in America* and its gay themes and brief nudity.

The Raleigh newspaper, in its coverage of the *Hollywood Reporter* story, dismissed Citizens Against Discrimination as "a 63-year-old retired man...sitting at home in the Henderson County community of Edneyville with a computer and an agenda....Regional film commissioners have never heard of him. Politicians have never heard of him. Area gay activists have never heard of him."

The head of the CAD contacted an attorney who wrote to the *News & Observer* requesting a retraction. The attorney called the *News & Observer* article "irresponsible" and "malice-driven," and pointed out that CAD would not release the names of its members for privacy reasons, not because those members do not exist.

The paper did not print a retraction and CAD filed suit.

The **Guilford County, North Carolina** board of commissioners became embroiled in a battle over taxpayers' support for theatrical productions that portray "an immoral lifestyle as acceptable." The chairman of the Guilford County chapter of the Christian Coalition had complained, "We feel it's not a job or function of the government to finance art." The Guilford commissioners cut all funding for the Greensboro and High Point arts councils in June.

While arts funding was restored two weeks later through a grant to the county school district, language deemed offensive by local arts advocacy and gay rights supporters remained. The resolution claimed that the United Arts Council of Greensboro had used taxpayers' monies for a "project which promoted lifestyles and values clearly contrary to those of the majority of the taxpaying public." The arts council had sponsored a community theater production of *La Cage Aux Folles,* a play about two gay night club owners.

Opponents asked that the language be stricken from the resolution. An advocate of removing the disputed sentence said, "You should remove it because it is divisive, because it is an affront to the gay community and their supporters and because commissioners should represent all of the people of Guilford County."

Others encouraged the commissioners to keep the wording in the resolution: "Some of you are sitting where you are tonight because you made promises to the Christian community to stand for morality, to stand for decency and to stand for traditional moral values."

The Guilford County board of commissioners voted 6-5 in October to remove the offensive language.

The **Mecklenburg County, North Carolina** county commissioners voted to ban funding of art that shows "perverted forms of sexuality."

The Focus on the Family magazine, *Citizen,* championed the vote of the county commissioners that "ceased taxpayer-funded sleaze in the face of media opposition and homosexual protests." The "sleaze" in question: the Pulitzer Prize and Tony Award-winning *Angels in America: A Gay Fantasia on National Themes,* which *Citizen* characterized as "a profanity-laced, homosexual-themed play," and *Six Degrees of Separation* by Tony Award-winner John Guare.

One commissioner proposed selling the Spirit Square center for the arts, complaining, "The majority of people who do most of the performing in that place are homosexual-type people, plain and flat simple."

The commissioners voted 5-4 to cut $2.5 million from the Arts and Science Council and barred funding for arts programs that "promote, advocate or endorse behaviors, lifestyles and values that seek to undermine and deviate from the value and societal role of the traditional American family."

> *"If the militant homosexuals succeed in their accursed agenda, God will curse and judge our nation. . . . The goal of the homosexual movement is to 'mainstream' unspeakable acts of evil... Their cries for tolerance are really a demand for our surrender. They want us to surrender our values, our love for God's law, our faith, our families, the entire nation to their abhorrent agenda."*
>
> Campaign literature for **Randall Terry for Congress in New York**

In 1998, a poll conducted for the Arts and Science Council found that well over half of those polled in Mecklenburg County would pay more taxes to support the arts, echoing the results of polls in 1996 and 1997.

A Charlotte resident protested an anthology of gay fiction available at the local public library before the **Mecklenburg County, North Carolina** board of commissioners.

The man read aloud graphic passages — complete with obscenities and explicit sex scenes — from the *Faber Book of Gay Short Fiction* during his three minutes of allotted public-speaking time. "It is criminal. It's hard-core pornography. It almost made me retch to read it," the man said. "To me it indicates they have lost control of the public library." The protester demanded the removal of the book and the firing of library staff responsible for the book's purchase.

Board meetings are usually videotaped to show later on the local government cable station, but the decision was made to pull the rebroadcast of the meeting during which the man read from the gay anthology.

OREGON

The widow of a popular **Oregon** author of children's books withdrew her support of an award named after her late husband because of the content of books vying for the annual award. The memorial award was to be given to a children's author during the Oregon Book Awards, but her husband's name was dropped from the young readers award prior to the November ceremony.

One book in contention was a "coming of age" story with muted gay themes. Although she claimed that her objection was not related to the homosexual content, the author's widow was unhappy with *What I Know Now* by Portland writer Rodger Larson for passages that she decried as "ugly." "I don't think there's a schoolteacher in this country who would stand up in front of a class and read this book," she said. "I couldn't stand by and have [my late husband's] name associated with it."

The endowment and memorial in her husband's name will now go to an award honoring state proponents of children's literature rather than one book.

A private school in **Corvallis, Oregon** canceled a scheduled performance by a lesbian duo after concert promoters refused to edit promotional material referring to the singers as "life partners."

The school's headmaster explained, "There was a question as to whether this is family-style entertainment."

The concert promoter filed a personal complaint with the city that the school had violated Corvallis's ordinance barring discrimination in housing, employment or public accommodations based on race, religion, age, disability, marital status, sexual orientation or source of income. The promoter argued that although the institution was a private school, by making its facilities available for non-school-related activities it was subject to public law. The school has since dropped its rental policy and suspended renting its auditorium while a new, nondiscriminatory policy is created.

TENNESSEE

A public library in **Nashville, Tennessee** asked a gay artist to remove two paintings from an exhibition after the library received complaints about the artist's sexual orientation and the content of the works.

One painting showed two men kissing good-bye in a restaurant; the other became controversial when a patron complained that he saw a penis in the work's heart design. The library eventually allowed the challenged works to remain for the duration of the exhibition, but canceled three subsequent exhibits while it formulated a policy on appropriate art for the library.

TEXAS

A magazine geared to lesbians and gay men will remain on the shelves of the **Lewisville, Texas** library. Local residents had formally asked that *Out* magazine be removed from the public library. "There are headlines of articles and descriptions of acts that are inappropriate for a setting with children with free access," a concerned parent argued. A subscription to the magazine was donated by an anonymous woman who requested that the library carry a magazine that addressed issues for gays and lesbians.

A library advisory board suggested that the city council retain the magazine. The board did not consider the issue of restricting access to the magazine, since the request was for removal. The city's attorney stated that removing the magazine would be censorship and a violation of First Amendment rights. The attorney's 15-page opinion stated: "Libraries are forums for ideas and information for everyone in the community and should reflect the broadest spectrum of viewpoints and ideas."

During the three hours of public comment at the city council meeting, opponents rebuked homosexuality as "not natural, not normal and not moral." Proponents defined the issue as "whether you will authorize a group of citizens who've appointed themselves as our moral watchdogs to determine what is or isn't available in the public library."

The Lewisville city council voted to approve the advisory board's recommendation to retain *Out* magazine.

The **San Antonio, Texas** city council zeroed out funding for the Esperanza Peace and Justice Center, which sponsors the city's annual lesbian and gay film festival as part of its diverse cultural programming. The conservative Christian Pro-Life Foundation mailed 1,200 fliers encouraging its membership to contact the council concerning the funding of the multicultural Esperanza Center, which it characterized as an organization solely of the "gay and lesbian community." The issue was also discussed at a Bexar

County Christian Coalition meeting. Esperanza was the sole arts organization to have its entire budget allocation cut; other organizations, including a gay chorale, were handed funding cuts of up to 15 percent.

Testimony at the public hearings was extremely critical of the lesbian and gay "Out at the Movies" festival sponsored by Esperanza. Brochure photographs — depicting lesbian couples and portraits of gay men — and festival film summaries were critiqued as "abnormal," "disturbing," "filth" and "borderline pornography" during the hearings. Denying claims of right-wing influence and homophobia, the San Antonio mayor and council members asserted that arts funding was reduced overall to accommodate other city services and road repairs. But the mayor told *The New York Times,* "[Esperanza] seem[s] to go way beyond what people want their money spent on. That group flaunts what it does — it is an in-your-face organization. They are doing this to themselves."

WEST VIRGINIA

A **Charleston, West Virginia** businessman, wishing to feature female impersonators at his primarily gay club, argued that city laws unfairly targeted his clientele. A city ordinance classified male-female impersonators in the same category — adult entertainment — as strippers and topless dancers, and required a special permit for businesses that produce adult entertainment. The club wanted to sponsor drag shows, but was not licensed for adult entertainment.

After two unsuccessful attempts to stage female impersonator shows under the old ordinance, the club owner appealed to the city's Municipal Planning Commission, requesting a change in the ordinance. Proponents of the change argued that support for the restrictions smacked of "gay-baiting and base prejudice." The planning commission voted 9-3 to remove impersonators from the adult entertainment ordinance pending approval from the city council.

"These shows don't involve nudity," *The Charleston Gazette* editorialized. "The city ordinance is outdated, and should be changed...." *The Daily Mail* disagreed: "The taxpayers of Charleston have a right to say where in their city they will allow adult entertainment. City Hall should stick up for the majority."

Thirteen city council members voted to amend the law, but opponents noted that a majority vote of *all* 26 elected council members was required to pass or change an ordinance. Not all council members were present for the vote so a second vote was scheduled.

A council member opposed to the revision complained in a *Daily Mail* letter to the editor: "For those who cannot innocently accept male-female impersonation, individuals seeking the change in the ordinance have established a posture of fear and intimidation." (The club owner threatened to file a discrimination lawsuit against the city.) The council member urged opponents to call the mayor's office and their council representatives to encourage a "no" vote on the ordinance.

The ordinance passed 14-12 with the mayor casting the deciding vote in favor of removing female impersonators from the adult entertainment laws.

MARRIAGE & FAMILY

The Right continues to beat its "family values" drum while denying gay men and lesbians any legal recognition of *their* families
and relationships. Claiming that loving and caring same-sex relationships somehow undermine the "traditional" family and that
lesbians and gay men are unfit as parents simply by virtue of their
sexual orientation, anti-gay leaders wage the battle in the courts,
in the legislatures, and in the media.

CALIFORNIA

A conservative group in **California**, Defense of Marriage, gained approval to collect signatures to get an initiative banning same-sex unions on the June 1998 ballot. The ballot initiative would define marriage only as a union between one man and one woman. A previous 1997 legislative attempt — the California Defense of Marriage Act (SB 91 / AB 800) — died in committee.

Defense of Marriage received authorization from the Secretary of State in August to begin collecting petition signatures. The Sacramento group had until January 2nd, 1998 to collect the 433,269 valid signatures required to get the initiative on the June 1998 state ballot.

But, according to a state lesbian and gay lobby group, Defense of Marriage withdrew its grassroots undertaking and is focusing on building support for any 1998 legislative attempts to ban same-sex unions and bar recognition of such marriages if granted in other states.

DISTRICT OF COLUMBIA

The **District of Columbia** agency charged with handling interstate adoptions has been labeled "extremely obstructionist to lesbian and gay adoption."

In August, a complaint was lodged against the D.C. Interstate Compact on the Placement of Children (ICPC) by a New York gay man who claimed he was unduly detained in Washington while "unprecedented" conditions were met, including calling the birth mother back in to sign another consent form. The man asserted he was held nearly two weeks and prohibited from leaving the city with the child he was adopting. During that time, his caseworker was repeatedly absent from work and an ICPC supervisor refused to take responsibility for the case or to discuss the matter with him or his lawyers.

"At best, I believe that there was incompetence and disorganization at play in this case," the gay man protested. "At worst, I believe that the possibility exists that we were discriminated against because I am a gay man."

In March, a Maryland gay couple was also delayed in the adoption of their son when ICPC refused to approve the adoption claiming that the state of Maryland would not process a joint adoption by an unmarried couple. Maryland finalized the adoption without delay. Currently, only Florida and New Hampshire bar gay adoptions.

The Maryland attorney who handled that adoption has since filed a complaint with the federal judge who oversees foster care and adoption in the District over what she called a "pattern and not just individual incidents."

"The office itself has been extremely obstructionist to lesbian and gay adoptions," charged the attorney.

FLORIDA

A **Broward County, Florida** lesbian couple was unsuccessful in an attempt to overturn a state law banning adoptions by lesbians and gay men. Their attorney charged the 20-year ban violated the state constitution's guarantee of equal protection because the legislature was trying to exclude an entire group of the state's citizens from being adoptive parents.

The state's witnesses said children raised by gay parents suffer emotional problems, fall behind in school and face ridicule from peers.

"The uncontroverted testimony is that children need both male and female influence to develop appropriately," the judge said in an opinion dismissing the class action suit. "[L]egislators were attempting to provide a complete family to children at a time when no studies were available to determine the long-term effect on children raised by homosexuals."

An attorney from the civil liberties group representing the lesbian couple protested, "This ruling substitutes anti-gay stereotypes and manufactured science for the overwhelming social research showing that lesbians and gay men can make great parents." The plaintiffs had called psychologists who testified to the success of gay parents, as well as gay witnesses who explained why they wanted to adopt.

"Take a Hike Dyke"

Title on an anonymous flyer distributed in opposition to a lesbian school board president who was running for re-election in the Wayne-Westland, Michigan school district

The number of children awaiting adoption in Florida continued to rise in 1997, while the number of people filing adoption applications continued to fall. Florida and New Hampshire are the only two states that prohibit adoptions by gay men and lesbians.

HAWAII

The decision by a **Hawaii** trial court in December 1996 in *Baehr v. Miike* that the state's denial of marriage licenses to same-sex couples violates the state constitution immediately unleashed an anti-gay backlash in the state legislature. Notably, the legislature in 1997 passed a proposed amendment to the state Constitution that would, if adopted by the voters, give the legislature the power to ban same-sex marriage (thus overturning the decision in *Baehr*), by "reserv[ing] marriage to opposite-sex couples." The proposed amendment will appear on the ballot in November 1998. As this report went to press, the state's appeal of the decision in *Baehr* was still pending in the Hawaii Supreme Court.

At the same time the legislature passed the proposed anti-same-sex marriage amendment, it approved a companion bill extending seemingly broad rights to domestic partners. The bill covered 60 items, from medical insurance to survivorship rights for "reciprocal beneficiaries." In practice, however, the law has proved to provide fewer real benefits than expected for lesbian and gay couples, and it has been the subject of litigation resulting in even more limited benefits. The law applies to any two adults who cannot legally marry each other, so includes, for example, two siblings, or a widow and her grown child. About one-fourth of those who registered as reciprocal beneficiaries are non-same-sex couples.

"The supposed innocuous pro-homosexual books are a Trojan Horse for the real objective — the indoctrination of and recruitment of young children. . . . Introducing and indoctrinating immoral behavior should not be a part of public education."

Citizen testifying before the Seattle, Washington school board in opposition to the board's accepting the donation of gay-positive books

The most significant provision in the law, mandating health coverage for the partners of employees of private employers, was stripped out of the bill as part of the settlement of a lawsuit over the provision. A federal judge, in approving a settlement of the case, agreed that the provision conflicts with a federal statute ensuring uniformity in employee benefit law from state to state. Five of the state's largest employers — Bank of Hawaii, C. Brewer & Co., Theo H. Davies & Co., Hawaiian Electric Industries, and Outrigger Hotels and Resorts — had filed suit challenging the mandatory coverage and then settled their case against the state. The settlement clarified the state attorney general's interpretation that the requirement to provide coverage for "reciprocal beneficiaries" applied only to companies contracting directly with private insurance carriers, as opposed to health maintenance organizations (HMOs) or member-owned group health associations (GHAs).

The settlement of the lawsuit did not affect public workers, who *can* obtain health insurance for their partners. Few public employees have taken advantage of that benefit, however, because they are required to pay the cost of the insurance themselves, and the public employee provision expires automatically in June 1999 unless the legislature extends it. One public employee stated, in reference to the status of the provision, "That isn't a guarantee; that's a gamble. It fortifies what we have said all along, that the only way to get across-the-board equal rights is through marriage."

Stephen Covey, best-selling author and time-management guru, was a featured speaker at a November fundraising dinner and seminar for "Save Traditional Marriage-'98," a political action committee (PAC) formed in **Hawaii** to oppose same-sex marriage. The PAC is dedicated to passing a proposed anti-gay marriage amendment to the state constitution in 1998.

"I am thrilled to be part of this tremendously important cause, and I congratulate you all for your efforts," Covey, author of *The 7 Habits of Highly Effective People,* told the Waikiki, Hawaii audience. "I believe it takes a mother and a father to produce a child and there's never been an exception. To me, that is kind of a natural principle for a natural law. And that's why I'm behind this kind of a movement." Prior to the event, a Covey Franklin (Stephen Covey's company) vice president told gay rights activists that Covey would not make any such pronouncements at the dinner.

The Covey spokesman later expressed regret over Covey's attendance at the event. "Our bottom line is we shouldn't have been there," he said. Covey Franklin also sent letters of apology to those national companies that had complained about the "unfortunate" appearance.

The state campaign spending commission has registered complaints against "Save Traditional Marriage" for fundraising violations surrounding the dinner and Covey workshop. Several attendees at the dinner and day-long workshop did not know their payments were considered a donation-in-full by the political action committee. A check from the Australian Consulate for a staff member to attend the events was returned because foreign contributions to candidates or political organizations are illegal in Hawaii. Another violation that could prove to be substantial is the in-kind donation by Stephen Covey himself. Covey did not charge Save Traditional Marriage for his services. Covey's speaking fees are estimated to be $60,000 and Hawaiian law limits PAC donations to $1,000 per person or company.

ILLINOIS

The Roman Catholic Archdiocese of Chicago responded quickly and negatively when the **Oak Park, Illinois** village board became the first municipality in the state to adopt a domestic partners registry. "[T]he archdiocese affirms its conviction that heterosexual marriage and family life is an essential building block of a healthy and well-ordered society," the statement read. "As such, it deserves to be both promoted and protected by public policy. Such protection implies, of its very nature, that no other social realities will be granted equivalent status."

The board's ordinance, adopted by a 5-2 vote, stated that "the village of Oak Park has an interest in supporting caring, committed and responsible family forms." Although the domestic partner registry does not provide any legal standing such as health benefits — Oak Park has offered domestic partner benefits to city employees since 1994 — backers say it is a symbolic step toward recognizing same-sex unions.

"It is not symbolic," complained one resident who disapproved of the measure. "The gay community has said it will pressure businesses and schools to enforce an acceptance. This is a tool to coerce and enforce acceptance." Other opponents voiced concerns that the domestic partner registry would send a wrong message to children and violate religious values. One feared the registry was "being sought as a proxy for gay marriage" and recommended gays seek therapy.

Opponents of the registry secured a non-binding measure on the March 1998 ballot polling residents of the near west Chicago suburb as to whether they want the registry. A majority vote supported the registry.

KENTUCKY

The **Kentucky** Court of Appeals ruled 2-to-1 that same-sex couples are covered by the state's domestic violence statute. The ruling reversed a 1995 decision in Fayette County in which a judge said same-sex couples did not qualify as "couples" under the law.

"This is a step in the wrong direction, especially in light of the very vocal demonstration by the gay community that they want the right to be married," said conservative state Sen. Tim Philpot (R-Lexington). "It's all part of the disregard and disrespect we've developed in society for marriage." Philpot pre-filed legislation for the 1998 Kentucky General Assembly that would limit domestic-violence protection to opposite-sex couples.

Earlier in the year, Philpot stated, "We need to remember that activities which many heterosexuals would consider aberrant forms of violent behavior, such as sadomasochism, seem to be more accepted in the homosexual sub culture ... I think we need to ask whether laws having to do with more clear-cut situations of women who are being beaten by men can be applied fairly to these other kinds of situations." Philpot's legislation would define unmarried couples as only "opposite-sex" couples under state law, leaving same-sex partners unable to secure court-ordered protection from an abusive partner.

In August, the Joint House-Senate Judiciary Committee heard testimony on Philpot's bill. Dr. Judith Reisman, a nationally-known anti-gay crusader and opponent of sexuality education, claimed that there are high rates of pedophilia and sadomasochism among gay men, while Louisville attorney Ron Ray discredited pro-gay testimony that day as part of a "very sophisticated propaganda campaign." The head of Lexington's Family Foundation noted gays would do for marriage what Dr. Kervorkian had done for sick people.

The Governor's Commission on Domestic Violence — chaired by the governor's wife — voted unanimously to oppose the bill. A statewide coalition of churches, women's and gay rights groups also stands in opposition to the legislation.

Philpot's bill was referred to the Interim Joint Committee on Judiciary where it died without action.

MARYLAND

The **Maryland** Court of Special Appeals overturned an April 1996 lower court decision restricting the child visitation rights of an **Anne Arundel County** gay parent. The original ruling forbade visits when the father's live-in partner or "anyone having homosexual tendencies or such persuasions, male or female, or…anyone that the father may be living with in a nonmarital relationship" was present. The appellate judges voted unanimously (3-0) that there was no evidence the children were harmed by the parent's sexual orientation or his same-sex relationship.

A local lesbian activist group had also filed a complaint about the lower court decision with the state Commission on Judicial Disabilities because Maryland's Code of Judicial Conduct forbids judges in their ruling to exhibit bias "based upon race, sex, religion, national origin, disability, age, sexual orientation or socioeconomic status."

The lower court judge who had issued the ruling said — despite the language of the written order and his signature on it — that the parent's sexual orientation had no bearing on his ruling. He sought to distance himself from the controversy, saying that he had neither written the order nor was he aware of its anti-gay language. The court order had been drafted by the mother's attorney.

MASSACHUSETTS

An organization of lesbian, gay, and bisexual parents, their children and friends was temporarily barred from participating in a community fundraising program sponsored by a **Northampton, Massachusetts** McDonald's franchise.

In June, Valuable Families received an invitation to participate in the community "Food, Folks, and Fundraising" program in which organization members staff the restaurant to raise money. Soon after arranging an event at the restaurant, the board chair of Valuable Families was contacted by the franchise manager. During the meeting it was explained that McDonald's would not "allow" Valuable Families to participate in an event at the restaurant because the organization was "too controversial." That decision, said the manager, was made at McDonald's corporate headquarters.

The group then scheduled a press conference under the "Golden Arches" protesting McDonald's discriminatory decision. "We are valuable families," a board member stated in announcing the planned press conference. "My children deserve the same support from McDonald's as any other child in this country." Several national organizations — Gay and Lesbian Alliance Against Defamation (GLAAD), Parents, Family and Friends of Lesbians and Gays (PFLAG), and Gay and Lesbian Parents Coalition International (GLPCI) — planned to join Valuable Families at the press conference. Minutes before the press conference was scheduled to begin, McDonald's regional marketing manager and Valuable Families announced the fundraiser would go on as planned with Valuable Families participating.

The regional manager said the incident was a "misunderstanding" and stated that McDonald's has a "zero-tolerance policy for discrimination of any kind." The fundraiser earned $400 for Valuable Families.

NEBRASKA

The **Nebraska** state court of appeals ruled 2-1 in September that a woman could retain custody of her daughter despite having had a lesbian affair. The woman denied being a lesbian, calling her gay relationship a one-time experience. Two members of the three-judge panel voting to continue the current custody arrangement expressed the view that there was no evidence that the lesbian affair had had any harmful effect on the child.

The dissenting judge, however, said, "With regard to this family's moral code, [the mother] has obviously set a horrible example. The record shows [her] conduct will necessarily impair [the child's] moral training. Therefore, it is in [the child's] best interest that custody be modified."

A local civil rights attorney said the judge was merely "imposing his morals" on the family. The attorney noted, "This is a case where at least two judges used common sense and acted rationally."

NEW JERSEY

The state decision allowing a **New Jersey** gay couple to adopt a child jointly was branded as "a loss for children and a victory for the homosexual agenda" by the anti-gay Family Research Council. Previously, state regulations prevented joint adoption by unmarried couples. The new policy resulted from the settlement of a class-action lawsuit brought by a gay couple who sought to adopt a child from the state's foster care program. The change also applies to cohabitating heterosexual couples.

Robert Knight, Director of Cultural Studies for the Family Research Council, criticized the mid-December settlement as "a victory for homosexual activism and a defeat for children already bruised in life and in need of an intact, committed husband-and-wife family." Knight claimed gay and lesbian activists are attempting to "redefine the family by pressing for homosexual adoptions."

"Children are too vulnerable and too precious to be used as pawns in the promotion of a political agenda," Knight said.

PENNSYLVANIA

A **Pennsylvania** lesbian won her three-year battle to have an **Upper Darby,** Pennsylvania cemetery honor its contract to have her partner's headstone inscription include recognition of their relationship. The deceased woman's contract with the cemetery stipulated that her headstone would read: "Beloved life partner, daughter, granddaughter, sister, and aunt." The deceased had given power of attorney for her surviving partner — not her blood relatives — to handle the cemetery arrangements for her.

But the cemetery claimed it was protecting the interests of the deceased woman's parents. The parents, who did not accept their daughter's homosexuality, requested the stone read: "Beloved daughter, sister, granddaughter, and loving friend."

After fighting the cemetery on her own, the woman approached a national gay and lesbian legal organization, which filed a federal lawsuit on her behalf. In an out-of-court settlement, the cemetery agreed to abandon its fight to block the inscription and pay $15,000 to the woman for emotional pain.

PUERTO RICO

Hearings on anti-gay marriage legislation in the **Puerto Rico** House of Representatives coincided with an international gay and lesbian conference held in **San Juan.** A member of the legislature filed a bill to amend the island's civil code to ban same-sex unions.

The author of the bill claimed it would "make it very clear to homosexuals that this society does not tolerate their conduct....This is a question of defending the morals and the values we are teaching our children." During the hearings, an Assemblies of God preacher brandished copies of *Daddy's Roommate* and another gay-affirming children's book, exclaiming, "Eventually school textbooks could be replaced to redefine the concept of family according to the homosexual community....No Puerto Rican in his right mind would be willing to allow such a minority group to impose books like these on our children."

Gay and lesbian activists attending the conference of gay and lesbian human rights organizations from throughout Latin America complained that the timing was coordinated to generate negative media about the conference, branding attendees as outsiders and "radical queers coming to change Puerto Rico." Conference attendees and members of a local gay civil rights organization staged an ad hoc protest march from the conference site to the capitol building.

TENNESSEE

A gay couple was barred from holding their commitment ceremony at a University of Tennessee campus chapel in **Chattanooga, Tennessee.**

The couple had registered — using only initials and last names on the registry — to have a ceremony at the university chapel. A university administrator learned the couple were two men when reviewing the application.

A month prior to the commitment ceremony, the school canceled the ceremony. University officials said the university and its chapel were bound by the laws of Tennessee, which do not recognize marriage between people of the same sex.

Tennessee banned same-sex marriage in 1996.

TEXAS

An **Austin, Texas** court of appeals ruled a lesbian was entitled to a trial in her lawsuit seeking visitation rights to her ex-lover's child. The three-judge panel based its decision on a state law that provides that such a lawsuit may be brought by someone "who has had actual care, control, and possession of the child for not less than six months preceding the filing of the petition." The court of appeals decision overturned the ruling of a lower-court judge dismissing the lawsuit.

A Republican state representative and same-sex marriage opponent called the appellate decision part of an ongoing battle over rights for gay and lesbian couples. "The mother that had the child certainly has all the rights any mother would have, even though she wasn't married," the representative said. "The fact that she had a lesbian live-in mate should not give that lesbian live-in mate rights to the child as if they were in a traditional married situation."

A Seattle, Washington lesbian became involved in a bitter custody battle with her children's father and his family in Texas. The woman and her children's father had been separated for four years and their twin boys had been living with her in Seattle by informal agreement. While the five-year-old twins were visiting their father in Texas, the father and his parents filed for joint custody of the boys, and the father refused to return the children to their mother. An **Austin, Texas** family court granted the father temporary custody — based on the mother's sexual orientation — pending a permanent custody hearing. The mother counterfiled for full custody.

After filing of the first round of court papers, the mother's Texas attorney withdrew from the case, leaving a message on her answering machine: "I think you need a gay-friendly attorney to represent you, and I'm not." The mother was beset by mounting legal fees.

> *"We have nothing against these people as individuals, but this is a family-oriented environment, and we do not believe that bringing in that type of activity is in keeping with our wholesome family goals."*
>
> Spokesman for real estate developers in Myrtle Beach, South Carolina, objecting to a local gay pride event

The executive director of The Lavender Family Resources Network, a national organization that helps lesbian and gay parents in general custody and visitation cases, commented, "So many times the relatives do not genuinely believe that the lesbian or gay parents are harming the child, but they will use society's prejudices in court to get what they want. And because litigation is so expensive, many decent parents can be defeated by bankruptcy as well as by homophobia." The Lavender Family Resources Network and the Seattle gay and lesbian community raised the necessary emergency funds to assist the mother in her court battle.

During the custody hearings, attorneys for the grandparents and father attacked the Seattle woman's "lesbian lifestyle" and alleged negligence. The judge awarded primary custody to the woman and ordered child support. In her ruling, the judge reprimanded the father's family for attacking the woman's lesbianism and urged them to stop interfering in her parental rights. The judge's ruling only afforded the woman temporary custody of her children through the school year; the father has requested a jury trial to determine permanent custody.

A Child Protective Services (CPS) employee in **Dallas, Texas** was reprimanded for removing a three-month-old boy from a lesbian couple's foster care without first notifying the foster home or the child's attorney. CPS returned the child to the foster home and demoted the employee for not following agency policy in removing the child. The CPS employee said she was criticized for failing to "exhibit respect to the foster mother who admits to criminal sexual conduct." Sodomy is against the law in Texas.

The employee filed a grievance over the demotion. In addition to her request to be reinstated to her previous supervisory position, she demanded that the agency adopt a formal policy against foster care placement with homosexuals. She claimed CPS has "a number of homosexuals in administrative positions" pursuing a gay social agenda. She further claimed that since sodomy is illegal in the state, CPS "as a government agency should not ignore criminal activity in the home." The woman's attorney from the Liberty Legal Institute, a right-wing legal group, said, "Apparently sodomy is the one crime that doesn't preclude foster placements."

The Liberty Legal Institute announced that the boy's uncle, now living in Chicago, had come forward to seek custody. The Institute had arranged for the uncle "to rescue the baby from a lesbian household." The uncle also has custody of the boy's twin sisters and three male cousins. CPS said the man had earlier declined custody of the three-month-old baby. The Liberty Legal Institute attorney said, "My client and I hope that no other child will be put at risk in that way again."

VERMONT

Three same-sex couples are fighting the state of **Vermont** for the right to marry. Two lesbian couples and a gay male couple who were denied marriage licenses in their towns brought a lawsuit against the state claiming that their constitutional rights to equal protection had been violated.

A group of gay marriage opponents, "Take it to the People," formed soon after the lawsuit was filed. The group is working for adoption of a state constitutional amendment that would define marriage as a union between one man and one woman. "The basic unit of social order in our country is the family, which is defined in the Judeo-Christian documents that our country was founded on as one man and one woman," a pastor and group member said. "Anything else would lead to social deterioration"

The state attorney general asked the court to dismiss the lesbian and gay couples' lawsuit. The state's 65-page brief argued that the state constitution does not guarantee same-sex partners the right to marry. The brief also stated that children have traditionally been linked with marriage and that same-sex partners cannot produce children without a third party: "Vermont affords marriage to opposite-sex couples, in part, because of the biological differences between the sexes that are necessary to propagate the species." The brief expressed concern that same-sex marriage could lead to an increase in artificial insemination and child custody battles. The attorney general explained that the statute's exclusion of same-sex marriage was justified by state interests in promoting the union of men and women, promoting child-rearing with both male and female role models, and ensuring that Vermont's marriages are recognized in other states.

The superior court judge dismissed the lawsuit. The judge ruled that there is no fundamental right to marry in the Vermont Constitution and that the discrimination against same-sex marriage could be justified by the state's interest in "furthering the link between procreation and child-rearing." One of the lesbian couples, whose own son died before the ruling, expressed their confusion at the decision: "We share the state's concern for promoting stable homes for children. In fact, part of the reason we sought to marry was to give our son the protection and security which came from having married parents."

The couples' attorneys have appealed to the Vermont Supreme Court. "Take it to the People" held a press conference asking the Supreme Court to uphold the decision. "I really feel that there are things in society that are important to preserve, and I think traditional marriage is one of them, " a leader for the group said. "It's a building block of society."

VIRGINIA

A unanimous ruling by the **Virginia** court of appeals reversed a lower court decision that restricted a **Richmond** lesbian's visitation with her son. The lower court ruling had barred any contact between the woman's partner and her son, even on the telephone. Since 1996, the lesbian, Sharon Bottoms, has battled for greater visitation rights after dropping a prolonged custody battle for the child. The woman's mother sued for and was awarded custody in 1993, after she learned of her daughter's lesbianism.

The woman's attorney applauded the latest order: "In reversing the 1996 order, the appeals court has seen through the cloud of anti-gay stereotypes and zeroed in on [the child's] best interests."

The appeals court wrote: "While issues of adult sexuality and related behavior are significant...such factors must be assessed by the court together with other relevant circumstances and balanced in a visitation arrangement which both benefits and protects the child." The appellate judges said it was wrong to bar contact with the partner solely because of her sexual orientation and ordered the lower court judge to reconsider the decision.

However, upon reconsideration, the lower court judge merely extended the woman's visitation but continued to bar any contact between her son and her partner. The woman's attorney called the new ruling "an outright defiance" of the appeals court order.

WASHINGTON

The University of **Washington** came under fire from a group of Republican state legislators for offering housing and health benefits to gay and lesbian couples. The Board of Regents had voted unanimously to open married student housing and eligibility in the school's health insurance program to registered same-gender couples.

"My biggest problem is that we have a state-run university that is promoting a homosexual agenda by elevating homosexual relationships to that of married relationships," one conservative state representative said. The Republican legislator felt that the Board of Regents "shouldn't be setting policy in the face of the values of the people of the state of Washington.... The people of the state of Washington don't accept homosexual marriage, either legally or morally," he explained.

Eighteen GOP legislators sent a letter to the University of Washington president condemning the president for what the legislators called his "blatant pro-homosexual political advocacy" and asking the Regents to reconsider and reject "this ill-conceived and socially irresponsible idea."

A poll of University of Washington students showed that seventy-five percent of them supported equal housing benefits for gay and lesbian couples.

EDUCATION

The public school has become a battleground over sexual orientation issues, as the Right fights to keep all mention of homosexuality out of the classroom, and many educators, all too aware of increasing harassment of lesbian and gay students, strive to teach tolerance and help students appreciate and respect diversity. Students in our public schools — gay and straight alike — continue to receive messages that hurt them. Lesbian and gay students are told that they are abnormal and perverted, and straight students are given a green light to belittle, harass and even physically attack their lesbian and gay fellow students. Nowhere is the climate more hostile than in the classrooms and playgrounds of our nation's schools.

An award-winning documentary about gay and lesbian issues in classrooms has incurred the wrath of Religious Right groups who denounce it as an effort to infiltrate schools for the purpose of "cynically recruiting a new generation to become homosexuals." In an August 1997 fundraising letter, Concerned Women for America (CWA) attacked *It's Elementary: Teaching About Gay Issues in School* (a documentary intended for adults and sometimes used in teacher training) for "methodically break[ing] down children's natural resistance to accepting homosexuality as normal" and promoting "ungodly and immoral behavior that leads to death." Focus on the Family's activist newsletter *Current Issues of Concern* castigated the National Endowment for the Arts' involvement in funding the "so-called educational film that is a brazen attempt to promote homosexuality to America's schoolchildren."

Robert Knight, cultural studies director of the Family Research Council (FRC), stated, "We think [the pro-gay message of the video is] a colossal lie and basically it's a way to teach teachers how to brainwash kids." Rev. Lou Sheldon of the Traditional Values Coalition (TVC) alerted his members to "stop the RECRUITMENT of our children" being "indoctrinated" into a "behavior that can kill them decades before their time." Dr. Howard Hurwitz, head of the Family Defense Council, claimed to be astounded that in his many years in education he had never seen "so scandalous a plan for indoctrinating children." Phyllis Schlafly's Eagle Forum charged that "[t]he video shows how psychological manipulation in the classroom can be used to change children's home-taught attitudes and beliefs about homosexuality."

> "I believe [lesbians and gay men] are a hate group attacking the moral fiber of the nation."
>
> Resident of Bozeman, Montana, objecting to a local gay pride celebration

Karen Jo Gounaud, president of Family Friendly Libraries, further sounded the alarm on the NARTH (National Association for Research and Therapy of Homosexuality) website, stating that "'Indoctrination' is not too strong a word to describe what [is] really going on..." in the video. She claimed that "homosexual activists...are successfully 'dumbing down' our ability to make accurate moral and socio-psychological discernments through their growing influence in government, business, the media and even religion." Gounaud warned that "[d]ecades of subtle and not-so-subtle propaganda materials, such as this video — and organized political efforts like the one that culminated in this film's distribution — have been stunningly effective."

The filmmakers have joined with the national Gay, Lesbian and Straight Education Network (GLSEN) to offer complimentary copies of *It's Elementary* to district superintendents and school board members so they can judge the documentary for themselves.

ALABAMA

At year's end, a state senator threatened to challenge funding of the University of Alabama Women's Studies program in **Tuscaloosa, Alabama** unless administrators addressed his concerns over the program. The senator charged, "They are promoting sex between women. There is a vulnerability with young women going off to college and trying to find an identity."

The department offers courses on such topics as women in the workplace, women and law, and women in the civil rights movement. Some classes have required reading lists that include lesbian issues and/or books authored by lesbian writers. The senator charged, "To have the most vulgar, nastiest descriptions of two women or more in bed with each other describing their body parts is not what academics should be about."

During the 1997 session of the Alabama legislature, this senator was also working on a revision of Alabama's ban on state funding for college gay and lesbian organizations in an effort to ensure that it could withstand First Amendment challenge. The original 1992 law was ruled unconstitutional by a federal appeals court earlier in 1997.

ARIZONA

A student columnist for the Northern Arizona University (**Flagstaff, Arizona**) student newspaper, *The Lumberjack,* wrote a column alleging that homosexuals are promiscuous rather than monogamous and "demand that sex with children be legalized." In a subsequent letter to the editor, the university's Lesbian Gay Bisexual Alliance (LGBA) protested the article's misrepresentations and claimed the "research" came from "an ultraconservative lobby organization."

The newspaper's editor canceled a follow-up article because she "didn't think it was fair and ethical" for the columnist to take the LGBA to task over their letter. "I just didn't want to get into a tit-for-tat."

The editor removed the columnist from the paper because she had distributed as leaflets copies of the article that was not published. University officials investigated the incident to determine whether the leafleting violated any University policies. The student columnist hired an attorney and announced her readiness to file suit if NAU moved toward disciplinary proceedings. The student defended the action as a free speech issue: "I wasn't attacking homosexuals. I don't agree with homosexuals. If you say anything against homosexuals, you are automatically called a bigot."

CALIFORNIA

In May, an **Alameda, California** elementary school teacher became the target of a parent's outrage over a seven-minute classroom discussion about an episode of the ABC television series "Ellen."

The father of an eleven-year-old student wanted the teacher fired for allegedly singling his child out and bringing her to the point of tears over her family's objections to homosexuality. The parent argued that school should not be involved in "social engineering" and that the discussion was in violation of written instructions given to school administrators months earlier that his child not be exposed to materials about homosexuality. "Homosexuality is immoral according to my Christian beliefs, and that is what my daughter has been taught," the father explained.

The family's attorney also filed a complaint with the California Commission on Teacher Credentialing seeking to have the teacher's license revoked. The attorney, associated with Pacific Justice Institute, a right-wing legal group, said, "Public school teachers must not allow any pro-homosexual agenda to infringe on the rights of parents."

The teacher had the support of the principal, and the Alameda Unified School District superintendent found that the teacher had not violated school policy since the discussion had been both "student-initiated" and "non-biased." The parents then appealed the decision to the school board.

In October, the board ruled unanimously in favor of the teacher: "The board has concluded that the parents' allegations were not supported by the evidence. No student was harassed, intimidated, ridiculed or intentionally embarrassed."

Finally, in December, the state Commission on Teacher Credentialing ruled that there was insufficient evidence to investigate the complaint.

The student now attends private school, and in April 1998 took part in an anti-gay Congressional briefing in Washington sponsored by Lou Sheldon and the Traditional Values Coalition.

The Laguna Salada Union School District and administrators were named in a lawsuit charging they failed to stop anti-gay slurs aimed at a **Pacifica, California** middle school student.

The suit claimed that teachers and administrators at Ortega Middle School were aware that the student was being "harassed, assaulted and battered and discriminated against...based on [other students'] perception that (he) was gay," but did little to stop the abuse, even after the twelve-year old sought help. The youth is not gay but acknowledged that he is more feminine than some boys. He reported continual verbal assaults from classmates including "faggot," "girl," and "gay-gay." "It's hateful to me," he said. "It affects how I feel about myself, my schoolwork, everything." The barrage of anti-gay insults and constant harassment led the child to suffer migraines, weight loss, eczema, asthma and even to consider suicide.

Frustrated after contacting school counselors, administrators and even the principal at Ortega, the youth's mother declared, "We went through all the channels...and hit brick walls." Counselors questioned the boy's truthfulness. An in-class training session was treated as "a joke" by students who were given 20 minutes to read a booklet that contained only passing reference to same-sex harassment. The student was instructed to report each and every incident to the school office, an implausible task, the boy claimed, since taunts often came from behind his back or from perpetrators well-hidden within the crowd of children changing classes; running to the office all the time just made him a pariah.

The student transferred from Ortega Middle School to Pacifica's alternative school where he said he feels protected and hasn't been harassed. The school board did amend the district sexual harassment policy to include sexual orientation.

The **San Leandro, California** school district came under fire from a conservative parents' group concerned with "decency in our schools." People Interested in Public Education (PIPE) was enraged by a lesbian science teacher who "came out" to her high school students and by reports of public same-sex affection between two students.

The teacher made the announcement to her class during a week-long lesson on diversity. PIPE demanded that the science teacher, another instructor and the San Leandro High School principal all be fired. The science teacher and second instructor are also faculty advisors of the Gay/Straight Alliance student club. "PIPE has an explicit agenda — they want to get rid of the gay stuff," said the other instructor, a heterosexual male.

Prior to forming the parents group, its founder had written to the *San Leandro Times* complaining that two girls had had sex in the high school bathroom and had not been reprimanded by school officials. The students denied the allegations — they had been caught kissing each other good-bye by a teacher who sent letters to their parents — and have since transferred to an independent study program due to escalating harassment at school.

"This is not about gay bashing," said the PIPE's founder. "It's about having decency in our schools."

People Interested in Public Education asked that the school board outlaw language and curricula that deal with "personal lifestyle choices" and reject a 1996 Alameda County Office of Education resolution that declared gay and lesbian students "at risk" and suggested that schools offer assistance to gay youth. PIPE's position is that it is not "academically acceptable" either to tolerate homosexual behavior on campus or for teachers to disclose their sexual orientation.

COLORADO

Twenty-two **Eaton, Colorado** high school students were suspended for organizing alternative events during their school homecoming week, including a "Diversity Day," recognizing people with non-traditional lifestyles.

The non-sanctioned events during homecoming festivities also included a "Safe-Sex Day" and "Gothic Appreciation Day," a day where advocates of the dark, brooding subculture would dress in black.

Public outrage erupted over the events that recognized gays and promoted safe sex. The Eaton High School principal acknowledged, "There was a tremendous outcry when the community heard what the activities were." The principal suspended the students, saying their events disrupted sanctioned homecoming activities and they had refused a school order to halt their plans.

The students felt their First Amendment rights had been violated by the suspensions. At an Eaton School Board meeting, one sixteen-year old complained, "I tried to raise social awareness and got suspended."

On behalf of the students and their parents, the American Civil Liberties Union (ACLU) of Colorado sent a letter to the superintendent of the Eaton school district calling the suspensions unjustified and unwarranted. The ACLU also noted that the principal had failed to alert the parents in a timely manner of the suspensions as mandated by Colorado law. The letter requested all suspensions arising from participation or support of the gay-affirming and safe-sex events be expunged from student records, that those students be permitted to make up all school work, and that a full and public apology be made to the students and their parents.

To avoid a costly legal battle with an uncertain outcome, the principal agreed to clear the suspensions from the student records and allow make-up assignments at full credit, but did not admit any wrong-doing and made no apology for the incident.

DELAWARE

A "wedding of friends" among **Dover, Delaware** elementary schoolchildren was challenged by parents who claimed it condoned homosexuality and promoted same-sex unions.

A supportive parent watched her seven-year old daughter exchange vows to play nice and promise to share with another girl and found the ceremony was "about friendship and friendship only." The teacher explained the ceremony was a creative way to get pupils to promise to care for one another as friends and was part of a larger lesson plan including a story about a West Indian wedding.

One parent claimed to be so upset with the mock marriage ceremony that she planned to home-school her son. Another parent expressed concern that the ceremony would send mixed messages to the children: "They might look back on it and it could cause some confusion later."

A conservative Christian group, ChildCare Action Project, charged the classroom activity "falls concurrent with the recent acceleration of the homosexual agenda to get laws passed to permit same-sex marriage." The group characterized the ceremony as "a play from Hell" filled with "value and morality modification" and "promotion of acceptance of homosexuality in public schools."

A school curriculum panel voted 9-2 in November to recommend that the school district make no changes to the class.

FLORIDA

Conservative student senators unsuccessfully challenged funding of the gay-lesbian-bisexual student organization at the University of **Florida, Gainesville**.

During a June allocation meeting, the student senate debated amendments by an Alliance Party member and an independent co-sponsor that would have slashed the $18,973 allocation for the Lesbian, Gay and Bisexual Student Union (LGBSU) to about $77. "It's important to realize that these amendments are rooted in bigotry," a LGBSU member pleaded before the student senate.

"I still believe that the practice of homosexuality is morally wrong," the Alliance Party senator said after his revisions were overwhelmingly defeated.

GEORGIA

In September, the state superintendent of schools publicly castigated the **Georgia** Parent Teacher Association (PTA) and its national office over its "liberal" focus and its support of tolerance for lesbians and gay students. She said, "I'm not in favor of that lifestyle, period. Particularly not teaching that in public schools."

Her comments came after her name had been mistakenly attached to a state Department of Education column extolling the virtues of the PTA and which quoted her as saying, "I'm a card-carrying member of the PTA and I hope you will become one too." She later distanced herself from the column: "I've never joined a PTA in my life. I don't want anybody to join the PTA." The superintendent belongs to the Parent Teacher Organization (PTO) of Columbia County, her home county. PTOs are not affiliated with the national PTA.

The Georgia PTA president announced that the National PTA (NPTA) has no official position on the issue of homosexuality. In an expose of the NPTA's so-called liberal and pro-homosexual agenda, *The Augusta Chronicle* singled out gay-positive passages in a 1994 National PTA / Anti-Defamation League (ADL) brochure and in "Talking with your Teen about Sex" (NPTA, 1995). After "properly" criticizing discrimination based on sex, race or nationality, the NPTA/ADL brochure "suddenly (and cleverly)" added sexual orientation to the list, the newspaper claimed. The *Chronicle* editorial then stated that the NPTA/ADL publication "concludes that parents, when talking to their kids, shouldn't be 'prejudiced' against a lifestyle condemned by the world's major religions." The president of the National PTA firmly stated the organization takes no official position on gay issues but supports the health and welfare of all students.

IDAHO

The **Idaho** Board of Education was sued in July for violation of the First Amendment when it denied a state university history professor a research grant because his subject matter was deemed too controversial. His proposed project was an exploration of the history of lesbians and gay men in the Pacific northwest around the turn of the century. The lawsuit came after board members refused to respond to a letter from the American Civil Liberties Union (ACLU) asking them to reconsider their April 1997 decision to reject the proposal. The grant proposal had received high ratings from a peer review committee. Another review committee also recommended funding the project.

"The pursuit of knowledge must not become victim to a popularity contest," said the cooperating attorney from the ACLU of Idaho. "The board acted out of the fear that some might find [the professor's] proposal too controversial, which is the same as allowing politics to determine what is appropriate for academics to explore."

The Faculty Council of Idaho State University in Pocatello passed a resolution saying that the denial was motivated by "an anticipated negative public reaction to funding a project dealing with homosexuality," and that the denial "produces a chilling effect on academic freedom." The nation's largest organization of professors, the American Association of University Professors, also sent a letter urging the Idaho Board of Education to reconsider its action.

The lawsuit was still pending at year's end.

INDIANA

A poster promoting tolerance toward lesbians and gay men displayed in a **Chesterton, Indiana** classroom became the focus of continued challenges by a conservative parent and a national Religious Right legal organization. The poster — which had hung in a high school English classroom for six years — features historical and popular figures including writers Walt Whitman, James Baldwin, Virginia Woolf and Edna St. Vincent Millay, along with a caption "History has set the record a little too straight ... Sexual orientation does not determine a person's ability to make a mark in the world, let alone make history."

The parent first complained about the poster to the school district's Materials Reconsideration Committee. The parent said the complaint was not directed to the gay content, but she raised a question as to "where it meets the objectives of the curriculum and where it fits in." She further stated, "I just don't think it's proper material that belongs in an English class." The review committee voted unanimously 9-0 to allow the poster to remain in the classroom.

The parent's complaint escalated. With *pro bono* assistance from Pat Robertson's American Center for Law and Justice (ACLJ), the parent appealed the decision to the school board. "This is propaganda promoting a homosexual lifestyle," she complained. "It is promoting coming out of the closet." The local Christian Coalition circulated a petition to have the poster removed. An ACLJ attorney argued that the poster violated state statutes on the teaching of human sexuality. "It flies in the face of abstinence," the attorney told the school board members. "The homosexuals on that poster do not by their definition engage in abstinence. The poster doesn't mention the risks to homosexual behavior." The board voted to uphold the committee's decision that the poster met curriculum standards.

But just before she was to announce the filing of a lawsuit, the parent decided to focus her energies on community activism on educational issues rather than file the court appeal. "While we could have challenged the school board's decision in court, we believe the most beneficial course of action is to encourage and mobilize parents in this community to become more involved in our education system — to take back control of raising our children," a prepared statement for the parent read. "This is not the end; it's just the beginning."

IOWA

The **Davenport, Iowa** school board voted 3-4 to reject adding sexual orientation to its list of classes protected from harassment. "The purpose was to let the people we employ and educate know that the Davenport school district is a safe place to learn and to work," said one board member. "They have a right to dignity. They have a right to feel safe. They have the right to not be afraid in our district."

Although the board members agreed that all people should be free from harassment and discrimination, some said they could not vote to add sexual orientation as a protected class before the city, the state or federal government moved to do so. Another board member said, "I do not want us to become known as the 'gay and lesbian district' across the state."

Bill Horn, the man largely responsible for distributing the vitriolic video, *The Gay Agenda*, has now set his sights on the National Education Association and has launched a promotional campaign for a new tirade on tape, *NEA: Abuse of Power*, designed to expose the "[NEA] liberal and strongly pro-homosexual agenda." Horn's Iowa Family Policy Center, affiliated with Focus on the Family, is located in **Des Moines, Iowa.**

Horn created Renew America, a tax-exempt non-profit organization, sponsored by the right-wing LifeLine long distance service, to promote the video and to educate America's parents on the education organization's alleged "startlingly aggressive liberal agenda." In the video, "ex-gay" Michael Johnston (Kerusso Ministries) and Carmen Pate from Concerned Women for America discuss the NEA's pro-gay resolutions. Horn told the *Des Moines Register*, "[The NEA is] in favor of bringing homosexual education into the schools, starting in kindergarten."

Other Religious Right organizations represented in the video include: Family Research Council, Eagle Forum, American Family Association, Coral Ridge Ministries, Liberty Foundation, Focus on the Family, Christian Coalition and American Center for Law and Justice.

KENTUCKY

After two months of contentious debate, the site-based council of a **Jefferson County, Kentucky** high school voted to keep controversial books by prominent gay African-American author E. Lynn Harris on its classroom shelves. The novels were removed after parents complained about the sexually explicit content. Members of local Religious Right organizations raised objections to teaching homosexuality in public schools at taxpayer's expense and called the novels "a recruitment tool for the homosexual movement."

Previously, a Jefferson County Public Schools (JCPS) committee had voted to retain the books at Louisville's Central High School as long as parents received a synopsis of a book and gave written permission for their child to read the novel. The committee's decision was sent to the JCPS superintendent for review and recommendation to the high school's site-based decision-making council.

Dr. Frank Simon, founder of Freedom's Heritage Forum and director of the American Family Association of Kentucky, and Peter Hayes, leader of the American Freedom Coalition of Kentucky, led an irate attack on the books. "First, they removed prayer and the Ten Commandments," Simon charged, "Now they want to teach homosexual pornography to 14-year-old children!" Simon urged viewers of his conservative television program to call the site-based school council to protest the books.

Finally, after a three-hour council meeting that turned into a shouting match between supportive students and protesters, the council voted 4-2 to keep the E. Lynn Harris novels available. Opponents held signs reading "Remove the Books" and "Porn No. Prayer Yes."

After the vote, Simon urged viewers of his weekly "Your Turn" television program to take the issue to the state legislature.

MARYLAND

Controversy erupted in **Frederick County, Maryland** when the school board-appointed Family Life Advisory Committee found two gay-affirming organizations — SMYAL (Sexual Minority Youth Assistance League) and Parents, Families and Friends of Lesbians and Gays (PFLAG) — listed in the forthcoming "Yellow Pages for Frederick County Teens." A committee member called for the removal of both phone numbers, claiming that SYMAL and

PFLAG promoted the "unsafe" and "perverted" homosexual lifestyle and were out to gain converts. The Family Life Advisory Committee voted 13-2 to include the numbers. The dissenting members then suggested adding three "ex-gay" organizations to the listings: Exodus International, Parents and Friends of Ex-Gays (PFOX) and the National Association of Research and Therapy for Homosexuals (NARTH). Their motion failed.

The associate superintendent of curriculum then approved the "Yellow Pages" with contact information for PFLAG and SMYAL.

A sixteen-year-old gay student was beaten and verbally harassed by a group of classmates outside a **Gaithersburg, Maryland** high school. The assault occurred in a school parking lot following an outside lunch break. The gay student was attacked as he walked away from a gathering of students who had been calling him "faggot" and "mommy." He was then pursued by members of the group, who caught him and then began kicking him around the face and head. The gay student suffered cuts and bruises on his forearm, hand, elbow and knee.

Montgomery County Police arrested a Gaithersburg High School student on charges of first-degree assault. The incident was the first reported since the Montgomery County school system added sexual orientation to its non-discrimination policy in 1996.

A workshop on tolerance of lesbians and gay men sponsored by a **Takoma Park, Maryland** Parent Teacher Association (PTA) was successfully presented amidst a controversy over its message. The workshop had come under fire from local anti-gay activists and a conservative newspaper as allegedly divisive and intolerant for not presenting any opposing viewpoints on homosexuality.

The organizers planned to show *It's Elementary: Talking About Gay Issues in School*, followed by a public forum. The announcement that all six members of the panel picked to facilitate the forum would endorse the "pro-gay" sentiment of the video enraged a local newspaper and parents who felt homosexuality is immoral. *The Montgomery Journal* complained about the video's "tactic of demonization" and also suggested its readers protest to Montgomery County school officials and demand balance at the forum.

A spokesperson for the Family Research Council called the video a "real slick propaganda tool on how to teach homosexuality in the schools." The vice president of a local parents group charged, "Support for the gays and lesbians is totally against what is a normal behavior for a child."

Organizers felt the public forum — even including a heated exchange with an "ex-lesbian" minister — was a good first step toward teaching children tolerance and respect.

MASSACHUSETTS

The student government of **Amherst** College in **Massachusetts** withdrew financial support from a conservative student newspaper for a myriad of reasons, including its having published an anti-gay satire. The school's Student Government Organization Recognition and Review Committee voted 6-0 to pull funding from *The Spectator*, claiming the newspaper did not comply with the committee's mission to fund "clubs and organizations it thinks will contribute positively to the campus."

The Spectator had published a "Celebrate Heterosexuality" parody of gay pride month activities. Many students found the issue offensive and homophobic. "We rewrote the gay propaganda they were distributing as straight propaganda and they didn't like it," the paper's founder and editor complained.

The newspaper was already on probation with the review committee over its failure to publish regularly and complaints about managerial and editorial policies, when the furor over the gay parody erupted. The president of the review committee claimed the editor was "trying to twist this into the silencing of a conservative voice. It's not; [*The Spectator*] is a poorly organized, poorly run organization that engages in irresponsible activities. That's the reason it was defunded." Another committee member remarked that *The Spectator* had overstepped "the bounds of appropriate behavior for a campus publication representative of Amherst College."

A seminar about "the homosexual agenda in our schools" was presented during a meeting of the Christian Coalition of **Essex County, Massachusetts**. The presentation was given by a Chelmsford public school teacher who is also the Massachusetts Education Specialist for Concerned Women for America.

The presenter showed excerpts from the video *It's Elementary: Teaching About Gay Issues in School* and talked about the "indoctrination techniques" used in Massachusetts public schools on the subject of homosexuality. "What I find troubling [in *It's Elementary*] is the equating of immutable, unchangeable characteristics, such as race or physical handicap, with sexual behaviors," the presenter stated. "Sexual behavior is always a choice unless you are a victim."

The presenter later stated that homosexual behavior results from molestation or rejection as a youth, but that many gays and lesbians can "leave the lifestyle."

Implementation of an anti-bias curriculum in the **Provincetown, Massachusetts** public schools was cast into the national spotlight by the right-wing media. The anti-bias project seeks equal treatment of all minorities — including those of race, religion and sexual orientation — in textbooks and class lessons. The project was misrepresented in a *Washington Times* story, head lined "Provincetown preschoolers to learn ABC's of being gay." In its story, the *Times* felt the need to describe the PTA president as a lesbian with a bi-racial child, "the result of [the mother] receiving sperm from a black man when she was artificially inseminated."

A representative of the Catholic Action League of Massachusetts, appearing on James Dobson's *Family News in Focus* radio show, stated, "Programs such as this aren't about promoting diversity. They're about enforcing ideological uniformity." He labeled the program another consequence of a statewide program to promote "gay rights."

Alerted by the *Washington Times* article, the Rev. Fred Phelps brought his Westboro Baptist Church to Provincetown. The Topeka, Kansas preacher, who is notorious for his anti-gay activity, including the picketing of funerals of AIDS victims, charged that the curriculum taught that "God is a liar, and that it's OK to be gay." Phelps also lashed out at homosexuality as a "filthy 'dumb brute beast' lifestyle" and an "abomination." His flier described the anti-bias program as "a milestone on the road to Hell."

Townspeople planned a peaceful response to Phelps's visit, wearing yellow ribbons. The 90-minute protest in Provincetown by Phelps, his grandchildren and other church members, was uneventful, with the vast majority of residents staying home and police protection out-numbering the protesters 3-to-1.

Soon after Phelps's protest, the Anti-Bias School and Community Project appeared to trade national controversy for internal struggle when a group of local residents organized as the Concerned Parents Group. The parent group expressed worry over the political ideology of some Anti-Bias Project members. "The [anti-bias] group is very politically active and vindictive," said an organizer who also called project members "intellectual snobs" forcing their own "intellectual bias" on the majority of parents.

The Concerned Parents showed their true colors during a November meeting of the Provincetown Parent Teacher Association (PTA). Approximately a dozen parents joined the small PTA at the meeting, quadru-pling its three-person membership. They then demanded that the PTA president, a lesbian mother, sign a letter to the school committee stating that the PTA does not want the words "gay" and "lesbian" spoken as part of a teacher's lexicon until the fifth grade. The president resigned in protest.

An Anti-Bias Project member said, "Those who demand and insist that the words gay and lesbian carry a strong sexual weight are themselves guilty of sex-ualizing gays and lesbians, an institutional practice that works to labels gays and lesbians as inappropriate and keep them invisible."

The school superintendent said any recommendation on the age-appro-priateness of certain words would go before the school committee no earlier than 1998.

MICHIGAN

A parents group in **Lapeer, Michigan** charged that an "unnecessarily explicit" textbook for ninth-grade health classes undermined the parents' religious teaching and promoted sexual activity and homosexuality. One parent argued that the textbook was "designed to lead students to view homosexuality as accepted and normal." The textbook was adopted by the school board in a 5-2 vote. One dissenting board member felt the text undermined traditional values with subliminal "hidden messages."

Soon after approval of the text, three residents filed a lawsuit challenging its adoption. At the request of the school board, the lawsuit was removed from Lapeer County Circuit Court to federal court. In addition, a dozen opponents of the health textbook — members of Family Action Concerning Today's Agenda (FACT) — picketed outside the Lapeer School District administration office, and another opponent formed a group called Concerned Adults Urging Scholastic Excellence (CAUSE) to raise money for a campaign to recall four school board members.

The **Wayne-Westland, Michigan** community school board voted 6-1 to rescind its earlier vote adding "sexual orientation" to the list of classes protected from harassment in the district's code of conduct.

The school board had previously voted in January to extend protection to lesbian and gay students and faculty. The school board president, a lesbian, then lost her re-election bid after anonymous, inflammatory anti-gay fliers — titled "Take a Hike Dyke" — claimed she would introduce gay themes and topics into the curriculum. The amended policy also came under fire from concerned parents during school board meetings.

> *"Anyone with any brains at all would know that gays are abnormal and against God's will....People like you don't deserve to live....Someone like you better watch out."*
>
> Anonymous phone caller in Stevensville, Montana, harassing a publisher of gay-positive books who had mailed book catalogues to school districts in Montana

An attorney for the school district explained that "sexual orientation" was removed from the policy to prevent possible lawsuits over First Amendment violations and free speech rights. "Districts can prohibit vulgar speech, but there are other comments about sex that aren't obscene, like 'I don't like homosexuals,'" the attorney said. "You can't have a policy that controls that kind of speech."

"This is an extremely sad day for people who believe in dignity and respect for all students and staff, because gays and lesbians in Wayne-Westland schools are now open to harassment, both physical and verbal," the former board president said.

NEW JERSEY

A former student filed a federal lawsuit charging anti-gay harassment at the **Sussex County, New Jersey** high school he attended. The lawsuit charged that neither the board of education nor teachers and administrators at Jefferson High School failed to stop the anti-gay harassment after it was brought to their attention. The gay man graduated from the high school in 1996.

The suit alleged constant indignities, including name-calling, spitting, shoving and, most seriously, a beating in his junior year that reportedly resulted in a loss of 80 percent of his hearing in one ear. The former student claimed teachers and administrators did nothing to discourage the harassment, merely offering the gay student a different changing room for gym class or allowing him to leave his classes five minutes early to avoid students who bothered him.

NEW YORK

A women's sexuality conference that included workshops on lesbian issues and was held at the State University of **New York** (SUNY) in **New Paltz,** was sharply criticized by state politicians and Religious Right groups. "Revolting Behavior: The Challenge of Women's Sexual Freedom" focused on a wide range of topics, including birth control, HIV education, homophobia, consensual sado-masochism and the use of sex toys. "Revolting Behavior" was the 21st annual conference sponsored by the Women's Studies Program at SUNY New Paltz.

A SUNY trustee called for the resignation of the campus president over the conference's "travesty of academic standards." The state Christian Coalition called the conference "profoundly disturbing" for "promoting sexual deviancy and potentially harmful sado-masochism." The executive director of the Christian Coalition of New York said, "This is not an academic freedom issue because this is not academic, it is organic — like horse manure." He then called on Gov. George Pataki to call a full investigation of this "abuse of taxpayers dollars." Pataki labeled the conference "outrageous" and pledged to "prevent this kind of activity from happening on a SUNY campus again."

The university faculty passed a resolution in support of the conference, affirming "the role of a public university in promoting open and uncensored dialogue and debate about controversial issues." The SUNY New Paltz president also defended the event in opening remarks at another conference a week later: "Using money or ideologies to hold ideas hostage is antithetical to the very nature of the public university."

A panel appointed by the Chancellor of the state university system to investigate the controversy absolved the campus president, saying the college was justified in hosting the conference and that censorship of the event would have been wrong. Critics on the board of trustees branded the report a "thinly veiled, but nonetheless blatant effort to quash justified criticism."

NORTH CAROLINA

A **Gaston, North Carolina** school board member raised concerns over a proposed health services program for youth, citing his religious views on homosexuality and other moral issues. The board was discussing the endorsement of "Straight Talk," a phone service with pre-recorded tapes on teen health issues, when the board member, who had been elected after a campaign in which he touted his conservative Christian views, launched into a 15-minute speech attacking gays, sex before marriage, and other behavior he deemed immoral. The board member explained, "Being in a healthy heterosexual relationship is the best way to avoid STDs."

The school board member was elected in 1994 as a member of Concerned Citizens for Public Education, a local Religious Right group.

OHIO

Religious Right groups protested the employment of gay men and lesbians in public education after a suburban high school math teacher was "outed" on a **Cleveland, Ohio** radio program. The teacher was appearing anonymously on the radio show as a member of the Gay, Lesbian and Straight Teachers Network. The gay teacher asked the host not to mention his school by name, but to describe him as a "teacher from a suburban high school." Unfortunately, the announcer mentioned the high school by name, "outing" the math teacher to a school official who was listening to the broadcast.

The official called the teacher into his office the next morning, solely to confirm the situation should the administrator's office receive phone calls about the radio show. No calls came in.

Still, Religious Right organizations were vocal in their opposition to openly gay and lesbian teachers in the public schools. The communications director of the Christian Coalition stated, "We are a pro-family organization opposed to any government-sanctioned approval of promoting a homosexual lifestyle. Especially given the enormous persuasion power that a teacher has in a public school or any school setting....To use public education as a forum to present [homosexuality as] an image of normalcy is not proper."

The executive director of Youth for Christ, a student ministry group, commented, "I believe that the homosexual issue is a moral issue and that homosexuals would like to turn it into an amoral issue — meaning nothing is right and nothing is wrong — and having an openly gay teacher promotes the desensitization of it as a moral issue."

Response among the suburban high school students to the outing of an openly gay teacher was low-key. "There's no difference in my learning...I don't think it affects the other students, either," a student at the high school explained. "[The man] is just our teacher; it makes no difference he's gay."

PENNSYLVANIA

A controversial book for gay teens will remain on the **Brownsville, Pennsylvania** high school library shelves. A parent had requested that *Understanding Sexual Identity - A Book for Gay and Lesbian Teens and Their Friends* be removed from the library.

Opponents complained about the book's descriptions of how to put on a condom and a fictitious seven-year-old boy's infatuation with an altar boy. One school board member labeled that excerpt as "church-bashing."

According to the school district's press release, a book review committee "unanimously agreed to keep the book on the library shelves with the option that if a parent does not want their child to take out the book they must notify the librarian."

"I'm against the book," a board member opposed to the decision announced, adding that if students "read one book — the Bible — it will answer all the questions they have."

UTAH

The **Granite, Utah** school board voted 3-2 to adopt a restrictive student club policy that effectively forbids the formation of lesbian, gay and bisexual student organizations.

The new "limited open forum" policy allows students to form extracurricular clubs only if they do not "encourage criminal or delinquent conduct, promote bigotry or involve human sexuality." In 1996 the state passed a law allowing school districts to adopt policies prohibiting clubs that promote "human sexuality" and criminal conduct. Sodomy is prohibited in Utah.

The school district policy was prompted by a request from a group of students to form a high school gay-straight alliance. The Granite school board chairman said, "This board is not prepared to spend one dime on litigation over clubs. Clubs are nice, but our focus is academics." A similarly restrictive policy enacted in neighboring Salt Lake City after student requests for a gay-straight alliance is now being challenged in court.

The policy adopted by the Granite board requires students to obtain parental permission before joining a club, restricts clubs of fewer than seven members, forbids any club titles that reflect human sexuality, and allows school principals to deny access by any club to the school newspaper, yearbook, bulletin board or public address system.

VERMONT

A sociology class at a **Montpelier, Vermont** high school came under attack from parents who felt a unit on human sexuality promoted premarital sex and homosexuality as acceptable lifestyle choices. The parents also complained about the sexually explicit materials used in the class.

The Washington Times reported on the parents' concerns as yet another example of the so-called "homosexual agenda" in public schools. The parents told the newspaper their daughter's class was given materials that suggested "'two lesbians make a more nurturing relationship than a heterosexual couple' because women are naturally more nurturing."

A review committee determined that the unit on human sexuality should remain a part of the sociology class, but urged the board to adopt a policy to provide parents with more information and oversight on any course that might contain sensitive or controversial materials.

High school students in **Rutland, Vermont** submitted a petition to school officials demanding they address the harassment of gay, lesbian and bisexual students. "We are tired of watching our friends get harassed," the petition read. "We are tired of seeing people depressed because they have no one to turn to. We are tired of students going to Rutland High School in fear and we want an end to it."

The petition noted that although racist and ethnic slurs were not tolerated at the school, teachers did nothing to stop the harassment of gay students. "Homophobia runs rampant at Rutland High School. The word 'faggot' is shouted in the halls every day and yet there are no repercussions. 'Dyke,' 'queer' and other such words and remarks, said in a derogatory manner, are used on a regular basis by students, all too often in the presence of faculty members who do nothing to stop it."

The principal had petition organizers meet with the school's faculty as the first step in addressing the anti-gay harassment. "Step one was to raise the level of consciousness," the principal said. "The next steps include some type of education for the rest of the student body and, beyond that, perhaps the community at large."

Two hundred students from the 950-student school signed the petition.

WASHINGTON

A gay high school student sued the **Kent, Washington** school district, alleging it did nothing to prevent and, in some cases, even promoted anti-gay harassment. The lawsuit contends school officials violated the gay youth's rights by deliberately refusing to provide him with a safe learning environment.

"[S]chool officials knew of the harassment and refused to enforce its own anti-harassment policy," the family's attorney stated. "For a six year period [the gay student] was a target of violence and harassment." A teacher allegedly questioned whether the gay student was qualified to donate blood because of his perceived sexual orientation, while another reportedly told the youth, "I already have 20 girls in my class. I don't need another." The lawsuit claimed continual abuse from students and faculty. A teacher first banned the young gay man from her classroom, then failed him, over his complaints about the abuse. The principal said the student brought the harassment on himself. Finally, the gay student was brutally beaten and kicked by at least eight classmates, yelling "faggot" and "queer," in a high school classroom as over 30 students watched, many actively encouraging the violence.

"We felt so hopeless," the young man's mother said. "We went to the school principals over and over for six years and nothing was going on. There were so many incidents. There was no response."

The lawsuit seeks to have the school district adopt and enforce policies that explicitly protect lesbian, gay and bisexual students from harassment and educate teachers and administrators to better address harassment and discrimination based on sexual orientation. "Every student has the right to go to school and get an education," the student's mother said. "They have a right to be safe."

Teachers, parents and health educators in **Marysville, Washington** are deeply concerned over a new district sex education policy that limits classroom discussion and information on sensitive issues such as homosexuality and abortion. The policy favors a fear-based, abstinence-oriented approach to sexuality education.

"I thought I became a teacher to help kids," a health teacher complained. "We're supposed to be preparing responsible citizens. But you can't be responsible unless you're informed." A parent called it "the meanest-spirited policy."

The new policy was adopted after a group of parents complained that a fifth-grade health book was too explicit and mature. A supporter of the new sex education policy said, "I feel comfortable with it because I don't have to worry about what horrid things are being talked about at school."

The school board president argued that limitations on discussing homosexuality were "not intended to be a denigration" and that the board would not "allow anyone to be disrespected." Still, the guidelines state that "[h]omosexuality shall be discussed only in conjunction with ... sexually transmitted diseases." The policy also requires that instruction not "promote" homosexuality.

A spokesman for the Washington Education Association, the state's largest teachers union, expressed concern that the policy may violate teachers' free speech and state laws prohibiting bias in curriculum. Others in the community have stated that they are willing to pursue legal action if enforcement of the policy actually results in restrictions on teachers' speech.

The **Seattle, Washington** school board came under attack by the Religious Right over the inclusion of gay-positive books in public school libraries. Funds to purchase the books — including titles such as *Daddy's Roommate, Daddy's Wedding* and *Heather Has Two Mommies* — were donated to the school district by The Pride Foundation and Fund for Lesbian & Gay Families with Children, a foundation set up by an openly lesbian Seattle council member and her partner. Critics claim that at least seven families have pulled their children out of the public schools because of the introduction of the controversial books.

Opponents have shown up at school board meetings carrying signs that read: "Shame is good" and "You need God." One woman berated the board for allegedly "promoting" homosexuality. "The supposed innocuous pro-homosexual books are a Trojan Horse for the real objective — the indoctrination of and recruitment of young children," she said. "Introducing and indoctrinating immoral behavior should not be a part of public education."

Another critic argued that the "books plant the seed for children to experiment with homosexuality, since being gay is portrayed as so fun, natural, better, the best way to be...while making traditional families appear unkind, too busy, angry, grumpy, boring, rejecting and unreliable."

An "ex-lesbian" accused gay parents of causing the harassment of their own children. "It is you who have subjected your own children to the pain of rejection by their peers," she said. "Your children didn't choose this. You did." She continued, "These books are tools and these children have became the pawns in the dumbing down of America."

Parents and Teachers for Responsible Schools (PTRS), an anti-gay group formed to oppose Seattle's safe schools project, led the attack on the books along with the Washington Family Council, a Focus on the Family state affiliate. A PTRS member dismissed claims of discrimination and harassment of sexual minority students. "There is very little to support the notion that there is an epidemic of violence against gays and lesbians in America," she said. "Their agenda is the introduction through curriculum of one side of a controversial issue denouncing all opposition as hateful bigotry, ignorant fear and blatant disregard of parents." PTRS members asked the school board to include books opposing homosexuality in school libraries and also requested that information about "ex-gay" counseling groups be made available to students.

The Washington Family Council urged parents to take action and prevent information about gays and lesbians from being presented in the public school. An article in their *Washington Citizen* publication, entitled "Affirming homosexuality: Coming to a school district near you," attacked the Sexual Minority Advisory Council and the openly lesbian Seattle council member, and urged readers to make their opposition to gay-positive curriculum known at school board meetings, Parent Teacher Association groups and to school principals.

The district's Comprehensive Health Education Office has received hundreds of positive calls about the books. A member of the original selection committee expressed confidence that school librarians were knowledgeable about distributing age-appropriate material.

RELIGION

One of the most tragic aspects of the hostility toward lesbians and gay men is their rejection by churches and religious denominations. In what for many is the major source of solace and nurturing in their lives, gay men and lesbians are unwelcome if they are honest about who they are. Mainline denominations are struggling over sexual orientation issues and, as that struggle goes on, many gay and lesbian worshippers are leaving the churches or hiding in the closet.

Right-wing groups including Americans for Truth about Homosexuality (AFTH) and the Family Research Council (FRC) protested a November 20, 1997 White House visit by openly gay Reverend Troy Perry (Metropolitan Community Church), dismissing the church's gay-affirming congregational message and claiming that the visit "further degrades the Office of the Presidency." Rev. Perry was one of some 120 religious leaders honored during an ecumenical breakfast at the White House.

Peter LaBarbera (AFTH) castigated Reverend Perry as a practitioner of a "subspecies of homosexuality which celebrates violent and degrading 'sexual' practices" who "champions the most vile perversions known to man." LaBarbera rejected the Reverend Perry's Biblical reading on homosexuality as "testament to man's infinite capacity for self-delusion."

Mark Tooley of the right-wing Institute for Religion and Democracy said, "It is highly disappointing and embarrassing that the White House should honor a church leader whose religious career had been dedicated to the legitimizations of homosexual behavior." Interviewing Tooley on the President's call for religious diversity and Perry's visit, Focus on the Family's *Family News in Focus* warned "the majority of radical homosexuals aren't in gay churches but are working from within to make all denominations gay-friendly."

Mere days after issuing a press release asking to put aside 'hate speech' in public discourse on homosexuality ("FRC Criticizes 'Hate' Rhetoric by Both Sides in Homosexuality Debate," November 10, 1997), FRC Director of Cultural Studies Robert Knight chimed in, "We are witnessing the Administration's moral meltdown. What's next? A memorial to Church of Satan founder Anton LeVay?"

By a simple majority, the Presbyterian Church (U.S.A.) passed a "Fidelity and Chastity Amendment" to its Book of Order. The amendment excludes gay men and lesbians and anyone sexually active outside of marriage from ordination or lay leadership positions in the church. Eighty-six of the denomination's 171 Presbyteries voted in favor of the amendment to the church's governance.

"It is truly a sad and tragic moment in our church's history," a co-moderator for Presbyterians for Lesbian and Gay Concerns said. "We are deeply disappointed and outraged that our denomination has chosen to make gay, lesbian, bisexual and transgender Presbyterians second class members. [This amendment] not only affects gays and lesbians, it affects everyone in the local church, including single and divorced persons, who desire to serve God, by the imposing of a purity code, unheard of since the Middle Ages."

At the denomination's General Assembly, a compromise substitute amendment was offered that called for "fidelity and integrity" in "all relationships." It was rejected by a majority of churches, leaving the more restrictive amendment in place.

Presbyterian churches in California, Delaware, Illinois, Ohio, New York, Utah, Colorado, Texas and the District of Columbia expressed disagreement and unwillingness to be bound by the new amendment by signing "Covenants of Dissent."

GEORGIA

Emory University in **Atlanta, Georgia** approved the performance of same-sex commitment ceremonies in its campus chapels, but enacted strict conditions on the new policy.

In June, Emory trustees temporarily banned all weddings from its non-denominational chapels until they could address a policy on use of university "sacred space" for same-sex marriages. The Board of Trustees' decision came after leaders of the United Methodist Church in northern Georgia criticized the Emory president for apologizing in May to a gay couple who were denied use of the Emory Oxford College chapel for a commitment ceremony. The church leaders complained that Emory, founded by members of the United Methodist Church, was obliged to follow a church law that prohibits same-sex marriages.

In an affirmation of the "intention for which Emory's chapels were built," the board voted approval in November of same-sex unions at campus chapels, but only if an ordained campus minister from one of Emory's approved 24 religious groups approved and conducted the ceremony. Currently only two of those denominations — the Jewish Reform Faith and the United Church of Christ — allow same-sex commitment ceremonies. "The practical effect is that it will make it more difficult for gays and lesbians; they'll have to jump through more hoops," said an attorney for the gay couple denied access. "What they're choosing to do is discriminate against gays and lesbians."

Although the new policy effectively bans most homosexual commitment ceremonies in campus chapels, those services still can be held in other campus locations, university officials stated.

INDIANA

Officials at the University of Notre Dame in **South Bend, Indiana** declined to add sexual orientation to the university's nondiscrimination policy and instead issued a "statement of inclusion" welcoming lesbian and gay students to the school. Gay students had protested the exclusion of lesbians and gay men from the policy.

The university officials claimed that they feared the presence of sexual orientation in the university's policy "might jeopardize our ability to make decisions that we believe necessary to support Church teaching." They further explained, "To make the change requested would mean that our decisions in this area would be measured by civil courts that may interpret this change through the lens of the broader societal milieu in which we live."

"We value gay and lesbian members of this community as we value all members of this community," the university president wrote in "The Spirit of Inclusion at Notre Dame," a statement issued to explain the university's decision.

IOWA

A Lutheran pastor in **Ames, Iowa** was barred from his ministry because, although church doctrine accepts his sexual orientation, he acknowledged being in a committed same-sex relationship. The Evangelical Lutheran Church of American (ELCA) allows homosexuals to minister, but only if gay men and lesbians take and keep a vow of celibacy. The church bars "practicing homosexuals" from being recognized as ordained ministers.

After learning of the pastor's same-sex relationship, the bishop of the ELCA Southeastern Iowa Synod asked the minister to resign. The man had been pastor of the rural Iowa church for 12 years. "My call as a pastor is to look out for the best interests of the church. I think the church is wrong and in need of reformation," the pastor stated. His congregation passed a resolution in support of him. None of the church's families left the congregation.

The pastor was called before an ELCA disciplinary panel, and after a two day "ecclesiastical trial," the panel voted to remove the pastor from the church's list of ordained ministers because he is in an openly gay, committed relationship.

The pastor has been allowed to continue his ministerial duties while his appeal of the decision is pending.

MASSACHUSETTS

Protesting Harvard's formal approval of same-sex marriage ceremonies at its chapel and the "pro-homosexual philosophy that pervades" the campus, a conservative university organization sponsored a "National Coming Out of Homosexuality Day" at the **Cambridge, Massachusetts** university. The Society for Law, Life and Religion of Harvard Law School, a Christian student group, was the local sponsor of the event, an "ex-gay" counterpart to the gay-affirming National Coming Out Day held each October. The mission of National Coming Out of Homosexuality Day is to offer homosexuals "a means to leave the lifestyle of self-destruction behind."

In July, Harvard began permitting gay and lesbian couples to hold commitment or blessing ceremonies at its Memorial Church. The president of the Society for Law, Life and Religion stated, "It was clear that Harvard had simply crossed the line in its embrace of the homosexual agenda. As one of America's modern cultural leaders, Harvard has a responsibility not just to its own constituents, but to that segment of society existing beyond the walls of Cambridge. By endorsing same-sex unions, however, Harvard has clearly abdicated that responsibility...." In a press release circulated by the anti-gay American Family Association, the club president further explained that bringing the "ex-gay" event to Harvard would begin a dialogue of hope and renewal. "It is time to break down the deceptive wall of rhetoric that precludes homosexuals from accessing the resources that could ultimately save their lives," he said.

Speakers at the event included "ex-gay" Michael Johnston of Kerusso Ministries and chairman of National Coming Out of Homosexuality Day, Robert Knight of the Family Research Council, Rev. Jarrett Ellis (King for America, a conservative group that claims that Dr. Martin Luther King, Jr., if he had lived, would have been opposed to rights for gay men and lesbians) and Jane Boyer, an "ex-lesbian" and founder of Amazing Grace Ministries of Portland, Maine.

Rev. Jarrett Ellis claimed that the gay rights cause does not qualify as a civil rights movement because "gay Americans tend to have higher incomes, better education and can be found in every level of the American economy and cannot point to any obstructions." According to Ellis, a civil rights movement is defined by "discrimination based on criteria that is arbitrary and irrational," but discrimination against lesbians and gays is done in the interest of "health issues" and the "protection of the traditional family unit."

Following the event, the Harvard Law School's gay and lesbian organization sponsored a "Speak Out Against Hate" gathering elsewhere on the Harvard campus.

MINNESOTA

Church elders prohibited a performer from singing at a holiday concert in a **Redwood Falls, Minnesota** church due to the man's sexual orientation. The gay man had been scheduled to sing at the Christmas Eve service at the Redwood Falls Church of Christ. The man had been baptized in the church and grew up in the local community, but had moved to the Twin Cities to pursue his successful career as a professional singer. He was returning to his hometown for the holidays and agreed to perform a couple of solos during the church service.

Days before the scheduled performance, the church's music director was told that the gay man would be welcome to attend services, but that he would not be allowed to sing. The church — not affiliated with the "open and affirming" United Church of Christ denomination — has a policy against gay men and lesbians in leadership positions. "They must have seen my singing as some sort of threat," the singer reasoned. "They must feel that by letting me sing, perhaps receiving some accolades, they would be showing they accept this [homosexuality] and that is not acceptable to them."

The man did not attend the holiday service.

OKLAHOMA

An **Oklahoma City, Oklahoma** minister left the Methodist Church because of complaints that she performed same-sex unions. The minister admitted to performing "holy unions" of same-sex couples at the United Methodist church where she was pastor. "I was told by the bishop I had to stop doing holy unions, or leave the denomination," she said. The minister said she could have requested a hearing but declined, feeling the process could be damaging. She said she felt "very strongly we shouldn't make people second-class citizens because of their sexual orientation."

The minister planned to start her own church affiliated with the United Church of Christ, which allows same-sex commitment ceremonies.

WISCONSIN

A statewide Religious Right group distributed fliers attacking an **Oconomowoc, Wisconsin** minister for his acceptance of gays and lesbians.

The anti-gay Wisconsin Christians United (WCU) distributed nearly 1,000 fliers claiming that the senior pastor of the city's First Congregational United Church of Christ "does not believe that homosexual acts are sinful and, in fact, believes that it is wrong to be against homosexuality!" The pastor was one of 85 clergy members who had signed "A Madison Affirmation: On Homosexuality and Christian Faith," a document declaring his support for an end to barriers against gays and lesbians in the religious community.

The director of WCU said the flier was distributed to educate the pastor's congregation. He said WCU's goals include educating the public about the "biblical and constitutional truth" about homosexuality, reaching homosexuals through the Gospel, and "to roll back the homosexual political agenda." "We want things returned to pre-1983 status, where sexual orientation is removed from non-discrimination laws, and we want homosexual acts outlawed," he said.

Wisconsin Christians United has used the same tactic with about 25 of the clergy members who signed the gay-affirming document.

GENERAL INTOLERANCE

From the workplace to state legislatures to neighborhood streets, anti-gay language and actions were in plentiful supply in 1997. Politicians clearly felt they could win votes with homophobia, Jews honoring victims of the Holocaust seemed to see no inconsistency in turning hatred against lesbians and gay men, and some Americans even resorted to terrorism to express their anti-gay sentiment. Make no mistake about it: the climate remains hostile.

American Airlines came under fire from national Religious Right organizations for the company's "sponsorship and promotion of homosexual activities." Leaders of four national groups — Family Research Council, Concerned Women for America, Coral Ridge Ministries and the American Family Association — signed a seven-page letter to the chairman of American Airlines' parent company asking that the airline cease sponsorship of pro-gay activities. Critics cited the airline's support of gay and lesbian pride events and political organizations, anti-discrimination policy in hiring gays, and marketing to the gay community.

The letter claimed that such public support for homosexuality hampered those wishing to leave the lifestyle through the "ex-gay" movement. The letter also rejected any comparison between the civil rights movement and attempts by lesbians and gay men to achieve equality. The letter stated that American's support of gay pride events constituted an "open endorsement of promiscuous homosexuality."

Gary Bauer, president of the Family Research Council, called American's pro-gay marketing and business policies an "open endorsement of sexual behavior that has been universally discouraged because it is immoral, unhealthy and destructive to individuals, families and societies."

Jim Woodall, chief executive officer of Concerned Women for America (CWA), stated, "This is an endorsement of a lifestyle that is deadly for the individuals involved. It tears at the fabric of our society — the institute of traditional marriage which is a union between one man and one woman."

"First, they removed prayer and the Ten Commandments. . . . .Now they want to teach homosexual pornography to 14-year-old children!"

Dr. Frank Simon of **Freedom's Heritage Forum/American Family Association of Kentucky**, during a debate over whether books by gay African American author E. Lynn Harris should be used in high school classrooms in Jefferson County, Kentucky

Soon after the original letter, the leadership of other Religious Right groups signed on to the campaign against American Airlines: James Dobson of Focus on the Family; Richard D. Land, president of the Southern Baptist Convention's Christian Life Commission; Ralph Reed, then-executive director of the Christian Coalition; Rev. Louis Sheldon, Traditional Values Coalition; and the executive directors of two "ex-gay" groups, Exodus International North America and Parents and Friends of Ex-Gays (PFOX).

Other grassroots groups signing the letter were Focus on the Family affiliates, including: Illinois Family Institute, Indiana Family Institute, Oklahoma Family Policy Council, Mississippi Family Council, Palmetto Family Council (South Carolina), the Center for Arizona Policy and New Jersey Family Policy Council.

The campaign escalated mid-year when the groups launched an ad campaign, placing an advertisement in several newspapers calling on American Airlines to stop what the Right called the "airline's endorsement of a radical movement that seeks to use government and corporate power to impose obligatory acceptance of homosexuality on all of society." The open letter again called on the airline to "stop lending its name to behavior that is immoral, unhealthy and destructive to individuals, families and societies."

American Airlines officials met with representatives of Religious Right groups in early 1998. The right-wing leadership characterized the meeting as a total concession by American. CWA claimed that the chairman of American had agreed that the "airline's marketing strategy was in need of change" and that it would no longer finance activities that promote "the homosexual lifestyle."

The airline denied that it had conceded anything to the Right. In a press release, American stated that in the meeting its officials "made clear that our objective is to provide quality air service for all customers and a discrimination-free workplace for our employees....[W]e have a strictly neutral stance with respect to lifestyle."

The chairman and president of American provided a more detailed account of the meeting in a letter to the airline's gay and lesbian employees' group, which read, in part: "American does not intend to sever relations with the gay community or organizations which represent it....Thus, we made it clear to our visitors [the Religious Right leaders] that we will make marketing and charitable decisions based on what is best for American, its customers, and its employees."

While American had already announced that it would no longer sponsor certain gay community fundraisers that had been controversial because of allegations of drug use and promiscuous sex, the airline stated that it will continue to sponsor AIDS service groups and events produced by the Human Rights Campaign and Parents, Families and Friends of Lesbians and Gays (PFLAG).

During August, the American Psychological Association (APA) adopted a resolution on "reparative therapy" for homosexuality. The APA, the world's largest association of professional psychologists, characterized such therapeutic approaches to "cure homosexuality" as unnecessary and ethically questionable.

Under the resolution, therapists using "reparative therapy" are required to read patients a statement declaring that homosexuality is not considered a mental illness, that other therapeutic options are available to help a person accept his or her sexual orientation, and that reparative therapy has not been scientifically proven to work and may cause side effects such as depression.

The response from so-called "ex-gay" ministries and supporters of "reparative therapy" was immediate. Charles Socarides, a right-wing researcher at odds with APA's gay-affirming policies and president of the National Association for Research and Therapy of Homosexuality (NARTH), called the measure "an attempt to brainwash the public" by denying that homosexuality is a "menace that is threatening the proper design of gender distinctions in society." Socarides pointed out the successes of his organization and studies supporting the therapy, charging the "[APA] have skewed the facts and given out a pro-gay program in trying to gain acceptance for homosexuality in this county."

Bob Davies, president of Exodus International: "People who want their behavior changed on pornography are free to go to psychologists today. Why should homosexuality be treated differently?"

Robert Knight, director of cultural studies for the Family Research Council, called upon the APA "to reject this disastrous retreat from sound clinical practice and to acknowledge the truth — that homosexual behavior entails inevitable physical and psychological risks and that homosexuals can change."

Soon after the announcement, "former homosexuals" picketed the APA national offices in Washington, D.C. Anthony Falzarano (Transformation Ex-Gay Ministries) claimed to be "very upset to think that the APA would even try to persuade therapists to outlaw this very important therapy." Falzarano — himself an "ex-gay" — labeled the resolution "a death sentence for those who are unhappy being gay."

President Clinton's historic appearance at a November gay rights fundraiser incurred the ire of Religious Right organizations and the conservative press, who attacked the Clinton Administration for embracing the "homosexual agenda."

"If the American people are shocked by all of the same-sex smooching that is on television, wait until they see an American president kissing up to the wealthiest extremists of the amoral left," said Andrea Sheldon, executive director of the Traditional Values Coalition.

Family Research Council (FRC) president Gary Bauer criticized the administration for "want[ing] the rest of America to put aside their moral-based objections to the gay rights agenda." Robert Knight (FRC) denounced the appearance as an "unfortunate misuse of the highest office in the land" and a "tragedy." Knight said, "To use the bully pulpit to glamorize behavior that offends the values of millions of Americans, behavior which is also unhealthy and destructive...is a disservice to the American people."

A handful of protesters outside the banquet carried placards reading: "Sodomy Brings Disease and Death," "Ellen Can Change," "God Hates Fags" and "Fags Doom Nations."

A Chattanooga Free Press editorial grieved that the President and Vice President "have ridden roughshod over sound, traditional moral standards and have affronted the majority of Americans" by embracing the lesbian and gay community as embodied by another honoree that evening, Ellen DeGeneres, "who has chosen to be a symbol of the attack on American morality."

Conservative columnist Linda Bowles and Empower America's William Bennett challenged the President's remarks that evening calling for civil rights for gay men and lesbians. Bennett wondered why the President did "not tell that influential gathering in Washington that so much of its misery has been self-inflicted." Bowles branded gays and lesbians as "a diseased community which wreaks havoc upon itself, blames others, seeks company for its misery and demands approval for its dead-end behavior." Both Bennett's article in the *Weekly Standard* and Bowles syndicated column then parroted discredited studies on gay mortality by Paul Cameron of the Family Research Institute.

In October, "Meet the Press" host Tim Russert asked Nation of Islam leader Louis Farrakhan to explain his recent comments that too many young black men were "turning homosexual."

"With the introduction of drugs and guns and the gang warfare, our young black males...are being turned into that which God had never intended," Farrakhan claimed. "...When you warehouse black men in prisons and they have a sexual drive that is being titillated by the lyrics and by the cultural degeneracy that pervades America today, this sexual need is sometimes filled by activity that God disapproves of."

Earlier in March, Farrakhan had made anti-gay remarks on CNN. He said that God "certainly...disapproves" of gays and that people "must speak against that which God himself disapproves."

A September fundraising letter from Concerned Women for America (CWA) attacked Rep. Barney Frank (D-MA), calling him "[o]ne of America's most notorious homosexuals...who clearly has no moral standards," and criticized him for introducing the "Anti-Hypocrisy Act of 1997" (H.R. 1915). Under the terms of the bill, consensual sexual activity between adults would not be a violation of the Uniform Code of Military Justice. CWA alleged that "this truly frightening piece of legislation" would decriminalize "adultery and sodomy" in the military. CWA Chairman Beverly LaHaye's fundraising alert rallied her troops to take a stand against the potential of "a sexual free-for-all, including aggressive predatory homosexuality and the spread of disease" which would hamper the military's readiness and further destroy morale. Donors and defenders of the armed forces were invited to request CWA's new report, "Surrender to Sodomy: Homosexuals and the Drive to Conquer America's Military."

President Clinton's nomination of an openly gay man, James C. Hormel, as U.S. Ambassador to Luxembourg drew fire from conservative members of Congress.

In November, soon after speedy approval from the Senate Foreign Relations Committee (chaired by arch-conservative Sen. Jesse Helms), two of the Senate's most conservative members — Sens. James Inhofe (R-OK) and Tim Hutchinson (R-AR) — placed a hold on Hormel's nomination. The hold blocks any vote on the nomination unless Senate Majority Leader Trent Lott (R-MS) intervenes. A spokesman for Sen. Inhofe said, "We just don't want the Senate's agreement to this nomination to be seen as agreement to a pro-gay rights agenda."

Similar fears were voiced by Sen. Hutchinson's office: "[Sen. Hutchinson] definitely has concerns about Mr. Hormel's activism." Even a December meeting between Hormel and Sen. Hutchinson failed to allay those concerns; instead Hutchinson announced opposition to the nomination.

Critics cited Hormel's co-founding of the Human Rights Campaign, an endowment gift for a permanent research facility (the James C. Hormel Gay and Lesbian Center) at San Francisco's main public library, opposition to the military's "don't ask, don't tell" policy, support for same-sex marriage, and a production gift toward making the film *It's Elementary: Teaching About Gay Issues in School.* Hormel said that, if confirmed, he would resign from the board of gay organizations and not allow gay groups to use his name in fundraising and promotional projects.

Senator Bob Smith (R-NH), who appears in an unflattering way in *It's Elementary,* became the third Senator to put a hold on Hormel's nomination. "This is not a tolerance issue," Smith said. "This is a matter of advocacy of the gay lifestyle." Smith also stated, "I'll filibuster until I drop before I let Hormel be the next ambassador to Luxembourg."

Lobbying against the nomination, the Family Research Council (FRC) stated, "We feel Jim Hormel, as a gay-rights activist, does not represent the values of a majority of Americans. His ambassadorship would be a slap in the face to Luxembourg, which is primarily Catholic." Government officials in Luxembourg, however, have told the Clinton administration they have no objection to the appointment.

When Congress resumed after its holiday recess, the Family Research Council went into full attack on the nomination. The right-wing religious group sent senators an information packet that attacked Hormel. FRC also asked its membership to call their senators in opposition to Hormel's "in-your-face radical activism that insults Christian and pro-family Americans."

"Respect for religious faith is at the core of what America stands for," FRC president Gary Bauer stated. "Appointing an ambassador who shows nothing but contempt for certain groups of believers should offend every American who believes in the Constitution."

FRC and the Traditional Values Coalition (TVC) circulated information to senators including a video of the Sisters of Perpetual Indulgence, a drag AIDS fundraising group who attire themselves as nuns, and a four-inch-thick folder of publications that allegedly promote "bizarre, immoral and illegal acts" housed at the San Francisco Main Library's Hormel Center. Hormel has continually stated he does not control the content of the library. Steve Schwalm of the Family Research Council disputed that reasoning: "So far, Hormel has not asked to have his name withdrawn from the material, nor has he condemned the material. He has washed his hands of it."

"The issue is Hormel," complained Andrea Sheldon (Traditional Values Coalition) who gathered the materials and pointed out the James C. Hormel Gay and Lesbian Center bookplates on the publications. "The point is that Hormel's name is on these publications." Detractors of the nomination also wrongly charged that Hormel's partner, Tim Wu, would act in an official manner as other diplomatic spouses do. Hormel told senators that Wu would not join him in Luxembourg.

"Provincetown Preschoolers to Learn ABCs of Being Gay"

Headline in the *Washington Times* on a story concerning a proposed program in Provincetown, Massachusetts designed to reduce prejudice and bias of all kinds in public schools

"I haven't declared [Hormel's nomination] dead," Senate Majority Leader Trent Lott said, but added that he did not see the Senate taking up the issue "in the near future."

Hormel was among dozens of pending Clinton nominees the Senate did not approve in 1997. A 1994 suggestion of Hormel as ambassador to Fiji was never forwarded to the Senate Foreign Relations Committee after concerns were raised by conservatives over the nomination. Hormel was also previously passed over for an envoy position to Norway.

Senator Lauch Faircloth (R-NC) fired his longtime pollster over reports that the pollster is gay. The gay man is in a committed same-sex relationship with two adopted children, yet worked on behalf of some of the U.S. Senate's most anti-gay legislators.

The pollster had previously stated: "I keep my private life separate from my business life — something my friends and clients understand, appreciate and respect." The conflict between the man's sexual orientation and his polling for anti-gay clients — including Senators Jesse Helms (R-NC), Faircloth, Bob Smith (R-NH) and Don Nickles (R-OK) — was noted in pieces for *Boston Magazine, Newsweek, The New York Times* and *New York Daily News*.

GOP sources reported that Senator Majority Whip Don Nickles also dropped the pollster.

ALABAMA

During a December television broadcast, the chairman of Alabama Gov. Fob James's re-election campaign and longtime **Montgomery, Alabama** mayor, Emory Folmar, used a disparaging term for homosexuals. Complaints from the local Parents, Families and Friends of Lesbians and Gays (PFLAG) chapter and Gay and Lesbian Alliance of Alabama found Mayor Folmar unrepentant. "I used the word 'queer' and I'll use it again. I'm not going to call them gay. I don't approve of their lifestyle one bit," Folmar reported to the *Montgomery Adviser.*

The mayor's remarks came during his response to a phone caller to "Good Morning, Montgomery" about being harassed outside a downtown nightclub. Folmar also recalled "I said something to the effect 'If you didn't all hang out together, there wouldn't be a problem.'"

CALIFORNIA

The **California** Supreme Court ruled that the Boy Scouts of America (BSA) may discriminate on the basis of sexual orientation and religion. The court held that the group is a private club rather than a business subject to the state's anti-discrimination laws and is therefore free to set its own membership policies.

The court issued a pair of decisions regarding the BSA: one ruling upheld a decision of a county scout organization in 1981 to reject an 18-year-old Eagle Scout as an assistant scoutmaster after learning that he was gay; the other ruling involved 9-year-old twin brothers who were barred by a county scout den in 1990 after they refused to declare a belief in God.

The California ruling is in stark contrast with an earlier decision [see page 123] by a New Jersey appellate court holding that the Boy Scouts and their local councils were "places of accommodation" with open membership and were therefore covered by the state's anti-discrimination laws. The New Jersey ruling was the first by any appellate court in the nation against the Scouts' anti-gay policy.

The Boy Scouts argued to the California court that homosexuality is inconsistent with the group's belief that Scouts must be "morally straight." Said one Scout leader: "We don't want them [homosexuals] in points of leadership. We don't want them, quite frankly, in our organization at all, but definitely not in points of leadership where these guys are scoutmasters."

Other similar cases are reportedly moving up through the courts in Chicago, Pennsylvania and Washington, D.C.

During his August broadcast, a Christian radio talk-show host in **Costa Mesa, California** suggested that homosexuality should be punishable by death.

Transcripts from KBRT-AM's "Crosstalk" program showed the host proclaiming that "[l]esbian love, sodomy are viewed by God as being detestable and abominable. Civil magistrates are to put people to death who practice these things." The announcer went on to urge listeners to contact their legislators to enact capital punishment for homosexuality. The station manager called the program "an honest dialogue concerning Christian beliefs."

The executive director of the Orange County Human Relations Commission (OCHRC) denounced the broadcast as a "thinly veiled call to violence" against homosexuals. The OCHRC passed a resolution condemning the talk-show host's language and also wrote letters of complaint to KBRT's owner and manager, as well as to the Federal Communications Commission. GLAAD (Gay & Lesbian Alliance Against Defamation) further suggested that Orange County residents alert advertisers to the anti-gay messages espoused on KBRT, remind them of the commandment, "Thou Shalt Not Kill," and propose that they take their business to a station more interested in promoting genuine Christian love and inclusiveness.

CONNECTICUT

Allegations that a nominee for head of the **Connecticut** Department of Public Safety had made anti-gay remarks played a role in the withdrawal of his nomination by Governor John G. Rowland.

The nominee, Col. William McGuire, had ordered a criminal investigation of an anonymous fax sent to the department's affirmative action office claiming he had made derogatory, anti-gay comments about a former state trooper who is lesbian. The woman had filed a discrimination suit against McGuire and other police officers. McGuire also ordered state police to investigate a Connecticut legislator who was critical of him.

The governor withdrew McGuire's nomination in December on the very day a second female state trooper filed a discrimination lawsuit against McGuire. Rowland said that although he believed in McGuire's professionalism, the state legislature was unlikely to confirm him to head the Department of Public Safety in light of the allegations.

A nurse with the state Department of Public Health claimed that a **Branford, Connecticut** AIDS patient and his male lover would "burn in hell" unless they became born-again Christians. During a home nursing visit, the woman told the couple that God doesn't like the homosexual "lifestyle." When the couple complained, the state suspended the nurse for two weeks without pay for "misconduct in [her] dealings with a homosexual couple," and barred her from any future home visits.

The nurse filed suit against the state over the suspension and a demotion in responsibilities. The American Center for Law and Justice (ACLJ), Pat Robertson's legal organization, represented the nurse and claimed she merely engaged the men in an amicable conversation about religion, and simply showed love and compassion by sharing her deeply held religious beliefs.

The ACLJ further alleged that the Connecticut Department of Public Health violated the nurse's rights to free speech and free exercise of religion.

The gay couple then sued the nurse for trying to force her religious beliefs on them, causing unnecessary distress and anxiety over her proselytizing. The AIDS patient called the exchange inappropriate and hardly amicable. "I considered myself to be a captive audience," said the patient, who lay in bed with a feeding tube in this chest during the hour-long visitation.

DISTRICT OF COLUMBIA

Organizers of a three-day conference on "Homosexuality and American Public Life" at Georgetown University (**Washington, District of Columbia**), sponsored by the conservative American Public Philosophy Institute, labeled homosexuality a "tragic affliction, with harmful consequences for both individuals and society." They maintained that they were trying to help gay men and lesbians escape a deviant and troubled lifestyle.

"This is not something negative," said the president of the group. He argued that acceptance and tolerance are no answers to homosexuality or the difficulties gays have in society.

Panelist Joseph Nicolosi, executive director of the National Association for the Research and Therapy of Homosexuality and advocate of so-called "reparative therapy" for homosexuals, maintained that "there is no such thing as a gay person," because homosexuality is "a fictitious identity that is seized on to resolve painful emotional challenges."

Nicolosi also argued that gay men are "disconnected" from other people and live in an unreal world. He said that is one reason why many gay men like theater.

Anthony Falzarano, another proponent of reparative therapy, was a featured speaker. Falzarano had been quoted on another occasion as stating, "Satan uses homosexuals as pawns. They're in, as you know, key positions in the media, they're in the White House, they're in everything, they're in Hollywood now. Then, unfortunately, after he uses them, he infects them with AIDS and then they die."

After protests by students and other community members that conference organizers were trying to represent their pseudo-science as legitimate academic thought by holding their conference at Georgetown, university officials attempted to distance themselves from the conference, saying, "We do not endorse the views expressed by the organizers or participants of this conference."

A former **District of Columbia** police lieutenant pleaded guilty to extorting money from customers of a local gay bar.

The lieutenant pled guilty to extortion in connection with a scheme to shake down men who patronized a gay film and burlesque theater in southeast

Washington. He also admitted to stealing $55,000 in police money — including federal funds earmarked for the witness protection fund — and engaging in wire fraud.

A man targeted by the blackmail scheme contacted the FBI. The FBI reported that the lieutenant had observed patrons leaving the gay club and used the car license numbers belonging to two of the men to obtain their identities. He then used police department computers to obtain additional background information on the men, including marital status, personal financial information and the name and location of their places of employment, and contacted them threatening to reveal their homosexuality unless they paid him $10,000.

Authorities stated that the lieutenant may have obtained additional large sums of money through other, yet-to-be-discovered extortion schemes against gay men.

Relations between the District police department and the lesbian and gay community had become strained over the police chief's so-called "zero tolerance" crackdowns on gay businesses. Activists and bar owners claimed the crackdowns were an excuse for police and city inspectors to harass and intimidate the businesses.

"Homosexuality shall be discussed only in conjunction with ... sexually transmitted diseases."

Sex education policy in Marysville, Washington school district

GEORGIA

Five weeks after the double bombing of a local family planning clinic, an **Atlanta, Georgia** lesbian nightclub was also rocked by an explosion, spraying four-inch nails and shrapnel into the crowd. Five patrons were injured. A second bomb was found in a backpack lying in an adjacent parking lot. Unlike the double bombing at the clinic, the second bomb did not explode. The mayor of Atlanta immediately ordered additional police patrols outside the city's gay bars.

Soon after the bombing, four Atlanta media outlets received identical, hand-copied letters claiming that the bombings of the women's health clinic and lesbian nightclub were carried out by "Units of The Army of God." The letter exclaimed, "The attack in Midtown was aimed at the sodomite bar (The Otherside). We will target sodomites, there [sic] organizations and all those who push there [sic] agenda."

In January 1998, a Birmingham, Alabama family planning clinic was bombed, seriously injuring a nurse and killing an off-duty police officer who was working as a security guard. In letters sent to Atlanta media outlets the very day of the Alabama bombing, "The Army of God" again claimed responsibility. Authorities warned Birmingham gay bars and gay-related service agencies to be vigilant about suspicious packages and strangers.

Following the mayor's request, the **Berwyn, Illinois** City Council set aside the recommendation of its Community Relations Commission to add sexual orientation protection to the local human rights act. The board instead adopted into public record a statement asserting that the current human rights ordinance is legal as it is now written. The director of the Cook County Commission on Human Rights said gay residents of the city are already protected from discrimination under county law which includes sexual orientation. Activists and residents had hoped the city would take a stand against anti-gay bias.

Some local lesbians and gay men expressed the view that no vote was better than a bad vote, adding that public opinion in the working-class town had been against the measure. Others, however, called the June non-vote "disgraceful."

The first proposal in the nation by a major municipality to honor the gay and lesbian community with a multimillion dollar street beautification plan has been met with controversy since its inception.

City officials and project designers in **Chicago, Illinois** unveiled their final proposal for a $3.2 million streetscape renovation for North Halsted Street, the business district of the city's heavily (though not exclusively) gay enclave. At the center of the controversy was a proposal to integrate two 25-foot-high neon-illuminated gateways and 200 pylons ringed with the gay pride colors along the streets of the ten-block area.

After several contentious meetings about the plans with area property and business owners, it was agreed that the neon-illuminated gateways would instead be installed in the central part of the streets and not be visible from the corners. Those compromises weren't enough for area fundamentalist Christian leaders, however, who vowed to rally their followers against the renovation plan which, argued one pastor, communicates to children that the "homosexual lifestyle" is acceptable. Homosexuality is a sin that the city is "forcing down our throats," remarked another Christian cleric.

The proposed renovations have been endorsed by Mayor Daley.

"We have definitely arrived," said the director of the city's Advisory Council on Gay and Lesbian Issues. "It (the proposed renovation) signifies to the community at large that the city recognizes our economic power," she added.

A **Chicago, Illinois** gay couple complained they were harassed by a security officer who objected to their public display of same-sex affection. The men reported they were sitting at the Merchandise Mart food court with their arms around each other and gently kissing. A security guard asked the couple to stop "carrying on" because other patrons found their behavior offensive.

The gay men protested that it was not uncommon to see heterosexual couples there behaving in the same affectionate manner. The couple then lodged a complaint with the assistant security director who wrote up a reprimand for the guard. Chicago's Human Rights Ordinance prohibits unequal treatment of gays and heterosexuals in places of public accommodation.

INDIANA

A gay group, Outspoken, was barred from marching in a **Fort Wayne, Indiana** summer parade at the Three Rivers Festival.

"Our parade is not a soapbox for people to advance a certain belief," said the Three Rivers Festival board president. "As a private organization, we have the luxury and the responsibility to make sure the parade maintains a mentality to keep it for the whole community."

Outspoken has been invited to apply again in 1998.

KENTUCKY

A proposed ordinance to ban discrimination on the basis of sexual orientation in housing, employment and accommodations was defeated for the third time in **Louisville, Kentucky.** Prior to the September vote, opponents claimed that the ordinance would create a "chaotic situation" in which the city would be forced to create new restrooms for transvestites and people would be prohibited from reading the Bible in church.

The chief opponent of the ordinance mailed fliers to his coalition members encouraging their attendance at Board of Aldermen meetings, and claiming a "major epidemic of sexual abuse of children by homosexuals." The flier read, "There are hundreds of children in America who are dying of AIDS because they were sexually abused by homosexuals." Local AIDS service agencies protested the opponent's erroneous conclusions and distortion of Centers for Disease Control and Prevention's information on teen AIDS infections and a 1989 medical journal article on the age of male adolescents' sexual partners. The author of the 1989 study complained that the anti-gay crusader had manufactured a "grotesque distortion" of his research.

Members of the American Family Association of Kentucky touted their poll which showed residents were opposed to "special rights" for homosexuals.

On the day of the vote, the streets outside city hall were filled with individuals on both sides with placards. The proponents' signs stated "Fairness Does a City Good" while signs of opponents claimed "Morality Does a City Better" and "Final Rites for Special Rights." Many of those protesting the ordinance had been bused in from an evangelical church outside the city limits.

Even after the ordinance's proponents on the Board of Aldermen had exempted churches and religious organizations from the hiring provisions, the ordinance still failed: three "yes" votes, seven "no" votes, with two aldermen — both supporters of the measure — choosing to abstain. As before, the Mayor refused to take a public stand on the issue. "Evil triumphs when good men do nothing," a saddened supporter complained.

MAINE

A special "people's veto" referendum in early 1998 gave **Maine** the dubious distinction of being the first state to nullify previously-enacted state-wide provisions barring discrimination against gays and lesbians in employment, housing, public accommodations and credit.

By a 52 to 48 percent vote, opponents of the gay rights law narrowly succeeded in what some observers have labeled a campaign of deception.

In October 1997, after the Maine legislature passed — and Governor Angus King signed — the gay rights measure, the Christian Civic League of Maine and the Christian Coalition of Maine announced that they had formed a political action committee to thwart the legislation. The committee, called "Vote Yes for Equal Rights," was the backbone of a Religious Right effort to have the civil rights measure repealed.

A total of 51,131 signatures, or ten percent of Mainers who voted in the last gubernatorial election, were required to put the measure on the ballot. The executive director of the Christian Civic League of Maine said that the 58,750 voters' signatures his group secured were a "miracle of God."

The effort to support the Maine civil rights legislation was led in large measure by Gov. King. During the referendum campaign, the governor was featured prominently in television ads pledging a vote against the proposed repeal of the statute. "Maine is a big small town," he declared in a commercial. "We know each other, we care about each other and we're neighbors in the best sense. And some of those neighbors are gay. But they're part of our community as well and deserve the same basic rights as you and me."

The effort to kill the sexual orientation statute was often augmented by paid visits to Maine by nationally prominent figures such as Alveda King, the niece of slain civil rights leader Martin Luther King, Jr. She protested any link between racism and homophobia when she spoke to gay rights opponents gathered at the State House in Augusta in early February.

Randy Tate, executive director of the national office of the Christian Coalition, was scheduled to join Ms. King at the State House, but had to cancel because of the weather. Prior to his scheduled visit, however, Tate commented on the referendum, "The issue of special rights for homosexuals now defines American liberalism as it moves into the 21st century."

Although Tate was a no-show in Maine, the national and state offices of the Christian Coalition played prominent roles in the repeal campaign by producing 240,000 "voter guides," that were distributed to more than 900 churches. The pamphlets posed several questions to readers that promoted a "vote yes" strategy to stir voter concern about the effect that a gay-rights law allegedly would have on children, and on a person's "right" to object to homosexuality.

Gary Bauer, president of the Family Research Council, also supported the people's veto effort and remarked after the election, "The spirit of liberty is alive and well in New England. This victory for Maine's families should give heart to all those struggling to maintain traditional family values in the face of liberal political activism. It means the people of Maine cherish the freedoms of speech, association and religion enough to fight for them in the public arena."

And Bauer reportedly sees the Maine victory as part of a larger national trend. "A fresh new breeze is blowing across America, with more and more people joining to restore and protect America's moral foundations," he said.

Governor King indicated that the fight was not over, however. "I think it's unfortunate," the governor said. "But we'll move forward. I think this is an evolutionary process."

MASSACHUSETTS

After Bell Atlantic was alerted by a **Boston, Massachusetts** gay activist to an inappropriate listing in its phonebook, the company announced that future Bell Atlantic Yellow Pages will not include "ex-gay" ministries among lesbian and gay services and organization listings. Beginning in 1999, New York and New England directories will list the "ex-gay" Transformation Ministries under the new heading of "Reparative Services" rather than under "Gay, Lesbian & Bisexual Organizations & Services."

Bell Atlantic's decision followed discussions with its gay employee group, Gays and Lesbians for Cultural Development. "Acceptance of gays and lesbians as healthy and as normal, both inside and outside the lesbian and gay community, is at the heart of defining ourselves as a community," the employee group wrote. "As gay men and lesbians, the idea that reparative therapy is in any way a service to the gay and lesbian community is offensive."

A gay couple in **Fairhaven, Massachusetts** filed suit in November charging their neighbors with harassing and threatening them because of their sexual orientation. The lawsuit alleged civil rights violations and sought unspecified damages for slander, invasion of privacy, and intentional and negligent infliction of emotional distress.

The lawsuit charged that the neighbors had circulated rumors that the gay men were child molesters and hung signs off their front porch, one reading: "Warning!! There are known homosexuals in this neighborhood. Watch your young boys at all times! They are looking for chickens." The gay couple heard taunts of "Faggot" coming from the neighbors' property and found a note on their patio table that read, "Go back in the closet and stay there." One of the neighbors reportedly told police that the gay men had molested her children. Her husband allegedly "barged" into the couple's house and threatened them, saying "I am going to kill you fags." Police escorted the man from the couple's house but no arrest was made.

The gay couple decided to file the lawsuit when the anti-gay signs appeared on their neighbor's house in late October. "It used to be that gays were embarrassed and moved," said a co-chair of the Governor's Hate Crimes Task Force. "Now, they stay and fight, determined not to go back in the closet."

A **Newton, Massachusetts** police officer retired from the force the same day he was to begin a one-day suspension for making an anti-gay slur. The police captain was suspended for one day without pay after Newton Mayor Thomas B. Concannon, Jr. learned of remarks the officer had made outside the mayor's office at a police promotional ceremony.

After a member of the ceremony complained of the heat, the officer reportedly said, "If the city didn't give all the money to the queers, the hallway could have been air-conditioned," making reference to a domestic partnership ordinance before the Newton board of aldermen.

"I am outraged that any city worker would use such hateful, bigoted language in a public place," said Mayor Concannon in announcing the suspension. On the day the 61-year old police captain was to serve his suspension, he turned in his retirement papers.

MICHIGAN

A December city council vote securing anti-discrimination protection for lesbians and gay men in **Ypsilanti, Michigan** proved futile after opponents collected enough valid petition signatures to force a referendum on the issue. The drive for the ordinance had begun after a local business refused to print raffle tickets for a gay student group.

A group of opponents, Citizens Opposed to Special Treatment (COST), was formed to object to "any ordinance that elevates a group to protect them based on sexual desires, sexual drives, and or sexual conduct." COST members felt the ordinance would "bully people who don't want to affirm the homosexual lifestyle." As passage by the city council seemed certain, COST filed two petitions with the city clerk. The first would place the ordinance on the ballot, while the second would amend the city charter to block the council from enacting any law that would extend minority status to homosexuals.

"From the fact that a militant, openly gay crusader is employed as Duluth's city planner... it appears that Duluth, Minnesota is another antichristic municipality going the self destructive way of Sodom and Gomorrah."

Rev. Fred Phelps of Topeka, Kansas, announcing his plans to picket in Duluth, Minnesota to protest the sexual orientation of a gay city planner

The city council voted unanimously to adopt the ordinance, and COST immediately began its petition drive. Early in February 1998, the city clerk certified the petition to force a ballot vote on the ordinance. However, COST had failed to identify itself as the group circulating the second petition, a violation of state law. Therefore, the second petition was not certified by the city clerk.

The city's non-discrimination ordinance was suspended pending the May 1998 popular vote on the issue. Less than a week before the vote, opponents held an "Upholding Christian Values" rally featuring Alveda Celeste King, the niece of Dr. Martin Luther King, Jr., and founder of the right-wing "King for America," controversial football star Reggie White, and gospel singers Debbie and Angie Winans. The rally benefited COST and a local ministers alliance.

Dr. King's widow, Coretta Scott King, sent a letter endorsing the ordinance to a city council member. "It's difficult to see how any reasonable or fair-minded person can want to repeal such a simple and just guarantee of equal protection under the law for all persons," Mrs. King wrote. "In a democracy, every minority has a human right to be free from discrimination, and denying this basic right to any group just doesn't square with justice."

The May 5, 1998 special election upheld the anti-discrimination ordinance.

MINNESOTA

Notorious anti-gay crusader Rev. Fred Phelps and his Westboro Baptist Church targeted a city planner and scheduled a protest in **Duluth, Minnesota,** which Phelps had characterized as "another antichristic municipality going the self destructive way of Sodom and Gomorrah."

The church's protest was planned in response to the openly gay Duluth city planner's publicly stating his beliefs that Phelps and his ilk had created "an environment of oppression" in Topeka. The planner had sought and was offered a job in Topeka, but cited Phelps's activities as his reason for declining the job offer. Phelps announced his planned demonstration outside Duluth City Hall in typical "fire and brimstone" fashion: "From the fact that a militant, openly gay crusader is employed as Duluth's city planner...it appears that Duluth, Minnesota is another antichristic municipality going the self destructive way of Sodom and Gomorrah."

Duluth's mayor countered the message of hate: "I'm a Baptist, I went to Baptist church for years, and that's not the kind of message real Baptists espouse. I don't think he'll draw much interest in Duluth." The city planned to ignore the protesters and their spiteful message, while other residents planned an expression of tolerance and love with a "Family Concert for Peace" elsewhere in town.

On the announced date of the protest, Rev. Phelps and his followers failed to appear. Duluth City Hall windows were filled with signs of the word "hate" crossed out. The "Family Concert for Peace" went ahead as planned. Church officials explained that the Duluth protest had been postponed until July 1998, to target the larger crowds anticipated at the city's annual "North Star Expo." The Westboro Baptist Church is still "determined to conduct a street-preaching mission in Duluth, Minnesota, in religious protest and warning to the citizens of Duluth that their municipal government was honeycombed with sodomite officials."

A bookstore in **Minneapolis, Minnesota** was the target of anti-gay vandalism in August. The front windows of A Brother's Touch bookstore were smashed with a hammer and the storefront littered with anti-gay and hateful epithets. "Fag," "KKK" and "187" (a police code number for homicide) were spray-painted on the building. In the next eight months, there were three additional acts of vandalism targeting the store.

The owner of the bookstore speculated that with increased gay visibility, "more hatred is coming out."

Police charged a Minneapolis man with the first act of vandalism, and he admitted damaging the property and spray-painting the windows.

A two-day lecture held in **Minneapolis, Minnesota** by Paul Cameron of the Family Research Institute was poorly attended. The lecture at the University of Minnesota was sponsored by Maranatha Christian Fellowship. The first session attracted about 100 people, the second day attracted a scant 15 attendees. "I guess people didn't want to come back and listen," said one campus pastor.

Cameron's discredited studies on the median age of death for lesbians and gay men (based on newspaper obituaries) and his "research" on gays disproportionately perpetrating child molestation are consistently cited by anti-gay crusaders and conservative "culture war" spokesmen as reliable information.

When his methodology was challenged by a university associate professor and psychologist attending the lecture, Cameron exploded. "You are being snowed by lazy, evil people on your faculty," he said. "They know it," Cameron complained. "They are damnedly wicked people."

A 50-year-old gay university alumnus who attended the lecture commented, "When I came here, I thought that he was going to tell me what a bad person I was; now I find he's trying to tell me I've been dead for 10 years."

Paul Cameron was expelled from the American Psychological Association (APA) in December 1983 for distortion and falsification of others' studies and employment of unsound methodology. Cameron admits he was under investigation by the APA in February 1982, but maintains he quit the organization in November of that year. The APA bylaws state that members cannot quit while under investigation. Cameron has also been censured by the Nebraska Psychological Association, the American Sociological Association and the Midwest Sociological Society.

MISSISSIPPI

A mental health counselor sued her former employer in **Tupelo, Mississippi** for firing her after "she refused to counsel homosexuals on maintaining homosexual relationships with other homosexuals." In her lawsuit, filed in Northern Mississippi district court, the counselor stated that she had said "she could not as a Christian encourage homosexuals to continue in the homosexual lifestyle" or counsel adulterers, and charged that her former employer, North Mississippi Medical Center, had violated her religious civil rights.

The woman had refused to counsel a lesbian client and her partner, claiming it would be contrary to her religious beliefs. The woman's attorney said the hospital responded that "that was not acceptable... [she] should be terminated."

The woman had complained earlier to the state's Equal Employment Opportunity Commission. That suit was dismissed when the EEOC was unable to substantiate that any violation of law had occurred.

MONTANA

The controversy over gay and lesbian pride festivities in **Bozeman, Montana** included a hateful flier from the Ku Klux Klan sent to the local newspaper claiming a threat of AIDS at the June pride weekend. The weekend events were sponsored by Pride! (Helena, MT) and the Montana Human Rights Network. The Klan's "Committee for Public Safety" urged residents to stay at home and avoid the festivities, claiming that AIDS could possibly be airborne and that residents should wear surgical masks if they had to venture outside. "Homosexual activists have been known to spit AIDS infected saliva and throw AIDS infected blood at counter protesters," the flier warned.

One local opponent paid for a newspaper advertisement reprinting the Pride! event schedule with the headline: "Is This What You Want for Your Schools Church & Montana? Just Say No To These Activities."

"I believe [lesbians and gay men] are a hate group attacking the moral fiber of the nation," a leading opponent of the weekend's events said. "I hate no one, I love the homosexual. It's the way they mock our laws that angers me." She and a dozen other protesters hosted a prayer service during the weekend's pride parade.

A Washington state book distributor of multicultural books received a threatening phone call, traced to a **Stevensville, Montana** high school, complaining about the gay and lesbian affirming books in her catalogue, and no action was taken against the caller when he was identified by school officials.

Soon after the distributor had mailed her catalogue — which included 23 titles that presented gay men and lesbians in a positive light — to school superintendents in Montana, she received the threatening anonymous phone call. "Anyone with any brains at all would know that gays are abnormal and against God's will," the male caller complained. "People like you don't deserve to live," the caller warned. "Someone like you better watch out."

The woman contacted the police and they traced the abusive call to an office phone at Stevensville High School. Although school officials acknowledged they knew the name of the caller, they declined to investigate or condemn the incident. "The phone call was mis-interpreted by the persons who got the call, and it's kind of been blowed [sic] out of proportion," the school board president said. "As a board, we decided to let it resolve itself," another board member said, explaining the decision not to discipline the employee. The board member stated she was "shocked that [books about c hildren who have gay parents are] being offered in Montana," and added that the school district wasn't "interested."

"There are hundreds of children in America who are dying of AIDS because they were sexually abused by homosexuals."

Dr. Frank Simon of **Freedom's Heritage Forum/American Family Association of Kentucky,** quoted in literature distributed in opposition to an anti-discrimination ordinance in Louisville, Kentucky

"Not being interested is one thing. Making threatening calls is another," said an organizer for the Montana Human Rights Network. "Kids who are thought to be gay or lesbian are already targets of vicious taunting in our schools," the organizer said, expressing concern for the safety of students questioning their own sexual orientation. "The actions of school officials have given even more permission to the gay bashers."

Local activists were outraged that the school board declined to apologize for the incident or discipline the Stevensville employee who made the call.

The director of the Women's Center at the University of Montana asked to speak before the school board at its next meeting. She was told by the board that she could not use the words "gay, lesbian, or homosexual" in her state-ment. "On a very basic level, this phone call legitimized the use of hate speech, condoned violence, and essentially gave a green light for anyone to threaten and even harm a person or group of people they do not like or do not understand," she stated. "Clearly, we cannot tolerate our educators set-ting examples of violence." The Bitterroot Human Rights Alliance also called on the school board to publicly condemn the threatening phone call.

A conservative school board member joined in the audience applause when an opponent of the controversial literature quoted from the Bible, condemning gays.

The local newspaper filed a lawsuit against the school board alleging that it had violated open meeting laws. The board's handling of the incident took place in closed-door sessions without proper notification, according to the lawsuit. The lawsuit is still pending.

NEW JERSEY

A **New Jersey** appellate court's ruling that the Boys Scouts of America (BSA) cannot discriminate on the basis of sexual orientation enraged Religious Right groups who charged judicial activism and "special rights" for homosexuals.

The appeal was filed in **Monmouth County** by a former Eagle Scout who was thrown out of the BSA for being gay. The former scout charged that the long-standing Boy Scout policy barring gays violated New Jersey's anti-discrimination laws. The BSA claimed it is exempt from the laws as it is not a public accommodation. In 1995, a Monmouth County chancery court judge ruled in favor of the Boy Scouts, invoking the biblical stories of Sodom and Gomorrah and criticizing the former assistant scoutmaster for his "moral depravity."

In March 1998, the appellate panel ruled in a 2-1 opinion: "There is absolutely no evidence before us, empirical or otherwise, supporting a conclusion that a gay scoutmaster, solely because he is a homosexual, does not possess the strength of character necessary to properly care for, or to impart BSA humanitarian ideals to the young boys in his charge." In a separate opinion, the dissenting judge agreed that the Boy Scouts had discriminated against the man due to his sexual orientation, but argued that the court did not have the authority to demand BSA reinstate the man to his former leadership position.

Reaction from the Religious Right was swift and decidedly alarmist. Robert Knight of the anti-gay Family Research Council (FRC) contended, "The New Jersey court decision compelling the Boy Scouts of America in New Jersey to admit avowed homosexuals as scouts and leaders victimizes the Boy Scouts and devastates the freedom of association in America. Compelling a private youth organization dedicated to 'duty to God and country' to accept individuals whose activities are in conflict with their moral values promotes neither tolerance nor diversity. It turns morality on its head, forcing an organization designed around teaching virtue to accept the values of homosexual activists."

Knight further charged, "the ruling shows how 'sexual orientation' references in government and business non-discrimination policies are being used to impose an extremist agenda through judicial tyranny." That same theme was echoed by his boss, FRC president Gary Bauer, on FRC's *Washington Watch* radio program. Bauer called the decision a "clear threat to traditional values" and pledged himself to ensure that "federal and state judges don't force the radical gay agenda on America's families and children."

The Christian Coalition decried the rulings as "an extreme example of the absurdity of legislation giving special rights to homosexuals." Executive Director Randy Tate complained, "This ruling underscores our concern with how the homosexual lobby is using bizarre and irrational legal theory to undermine morals which parents instill in their children."

The BSA faces an additional anti-discrimination battle in the District of Columbia. Shortly after the New Jersey ruling, the state supreme court in California ruled that the BSA is a private organization and may discriminate on the basis of religion or sexual orientation. [See page 110.]

A direct mail piece from *Randall Terry for Congress* attacked the incumbent Representative for his support of same-sex marriage and the "homosexual agenda." Anti-abortion crusader Randall Terry seeks to represent the 26th District of New York. The December fundraising letter branded incumbent Rep. Maurice Hinchey (D-NY) as "part of a growing number of treacherous congressmen who support special rights for homosexuals" and promote "this horrifying 'death-style' to teenagers." Hinchey's vote against the Defense of Marriage Act (DOMA) was miscast as a vote supporting federal recognition of same-sex marriage, a "deplorable, treacherous abomination against God and men." The letter labeled DOMA as a "hideous bill."

Terry claimed that he was the target of death threats due to his strong anti-abortion beliefs and for "fighting with all my heart against those who want to legalize homosexual marriage." "We are fighting for the very survival of America," Terry wrote. "If the militant homosexuals succeed in the accursed agenda, God will curse and judge our nation."

"The goal of the homosexual movement is to 'mainstream' unspeakable acts of evil... Their cries for tolerance are really a demand for our surrender. They want us to surrender our values, our love for God's law, our faith, our families, the entire nation to their abhorrent agenda," the letter claimed. "We can never tolerate that which brings the judgment of God on our nation and chaos to our families."

The fundraising letter closed with Terry's request for prayers and gifts of $20 to $750 to be used to fund a "prophetic wave of political ads" against the incumbent's "promotion of homosexual marriage, forced abortion in China and oppressive taxes."

A **New York City** police officer was reprimanded over "a host of vulgar and highly offensive statements" he allegedly made while returning a medal of valor given to him by a gay police officers group.

The Gay Officers Action League (GOAL) had presented a medal to the officer at a Police Department's Medal Day awards ceremony. Immediately following the ceremony, the officer removed the medal from his chest, handed it back to the GOAL president and told him to "shove it up [the GOAL president's] ass and then shove it up the asses of the thousand members of GOAL." The GOAL president said, "It was one of the most homophobic incidents I've ever witnessed in my career."

The officer was suspended for 30 days without pay.

Conservative Jewish groups and anti-gay activists protested the inclusion of exhibits about or mention of lesbians and gay men in the new Museum of Jewish Heritage, even filing a lawsuit to stop the September opening of the **New York City** Holocaust museum.

An issue of *Jewish Week* quoted several people protesting at the museum site in Battery Park who expressed their belief that homosexuals were not victims, but instead perpetrators of the Nazi regime. Howard Hurwitz, chairman of the Family Defense Council, expressed the view that for the new museum to include recognition of gay Holocaust victims was "not a revision of history but a total falsification." "The purpose of a Holocaust memorial is emphasizing the persecution of Jews," an Orthodox rabbi was quoted as stating. "To utilize it as something else is sacrilege."

Exposing "The Truth About Homosexuals and the Holocaust" in *Human Events*, Hurwitz called the recognition of gays at the New York museum an "obscenity" that "perpetuate[s] the myth that homosexuals were the 'victims' of the Nazis." Hurwitz claims that homosexuals were founders of the Nazi Party and warned, "Inclusion of homosexuals as 'victims' in Holocaust museums is contributing to the growing decadence that imperils traditional family values in our country."

The Rabbinical Alliance of America pledged to boycott the Holocaust museum if any mention of homosexuals were included.

Sixteen Orthodox Jewish rabbis filed a lawsuit to stop the opening of the Museum of Jewish Heritage because it included an exhibit honoring lesbians and gay men who were persecuted by the Nazis. The lead plaintiff complained about "the elevation of homosexuals to the martyred status of the six million Jews" who perished in the Holocaust. "It is callous and outrageous to use something as sacred as the Holocaust as a means of achieving the political goals of the militant homosexual community," he insisted. The suit says the use of public money to build the museum was unconstitutional.

The Museum of Jewish Heritage opened on schedule. Acknowledgment of gay victims of the Holocaust is minimal: a pink triangle, a timeline that notes when gays were incarcerated, and a videotape interview with a camp survivor mentioning that Hitler also targeted gays for arrest.

Gays and lesbians were once again barred from marching in the annual India Day Parade in **New York City.** The South Asian Lesbian and Gay Association (SALGA) has petitioned the parade organizers, the Federation of Indian Associations, for permission to march since 1992. That year a SALGA contingent did march after the city's human rights commissioner negotiated with the organizers to allow the lesbian and gay group to participate. The annual parade commemorates the anniversary of India's independence from British colonial rule.

The **Orangetown, New York** Republican Committee removed an incumbent town board member from its November slate of candidates because of her "extracurricular" activities in support of gay civil rights. Local Republicans were distressed by the woman's involvement with local chapters of Parents, Families and Friends of Lesbians and Gays (PFLAG) and her volunteer work with a support organization that provides hot meals to homebound people with AIDS.

The vice chair of the Rockland Anti-Bias Commission said, "It proves that there are certainly members in power who feel that it is OK to discriminate openly, not just against gays, but against people who *support* gays."

NORTH CAROLINA

A group of **Asheville, North Carolina** ministers expressed public concern over an announced 1998 gay pride march in the city. The ministers had staged a counter march celebrating family values in 1992 one week after that year's gay and lesbian parade. "I do not think it is good for our city or our community to have a parade for any type of bad behavior," a local Baptist pastor said. "We would not want a parade for thieves or people who rob banks or a parade for adulterers, homosexuals or lesbian lifestyles. It is wrong I believe to parade sin."

The pastor questioned a civil rights march in celebration of homosexuality: "Sin is not a civil right. I believe it is an affront to the black community and to the Hispanic and Jewish communities and to our female population to equate homosexuality to true minorities. Homosexuality is still against the law in North Carolina and a law of God. It is a sin of choice." Another pastor stated, "A minority is a minority from birth and not by choice."

March organizers estimate 6,000 people will attend the June 1998 state gay pride march in Asheville.

Until it was challenged, the Internal Revenue Service (IRS) seemed ready to deny tax-exempt status to a **Greensboro, North Carolina** gay youth group because of concerns that the group did not sufficiently discourage the "development of homosexual attitudes and propensities by the young and impressionable."

The Gay and Lesbian Adolescent Support System (GLASS) applied for tax-exempt status in 1996 and received a letter from the IRS requesting that it "detail the procedures and safeguards in place to assure counselors and participants do not encourage or facilitate homosexual practices or encourage the development of homosexual attitudes and propensities by minor individuals attending your program." GLASS contacted the Lambda Legal Defense and Education Fund and a Lambda attorney challenged the IRS. In his letter, the attorney objected to the "antagonistic treatment" by the federal government of the youth group and "negative judgment about our client's viewpoint and the gay sexual orientation of those it serves." Lambda's attorney also argued that the IRS had no business inquiring about "homosexual attitudes," since it never inquires about "heterosexual attitudes."

Acknowledging that it was wrong to police the gay youth group's viewpoint, the IRS withdrew its 1996 letter and re-opened the case. The IRS granted GLASS the tax exemption "based on the information supplied," and declined to comment further on the case.

Right-wing **Mecklenburg County, North Carolina** commissioners ousted their chairman because of his support for a gay political candidate.

A conservative Democratic commissioner — who had been instrumental in the board's move to cut county arts funding over issues of homosexuality — lambasted the Democratic chairman over his "quest to glorify a homosexual candidate." The commissioner complained, "There are some potentially good candidates — black, white and Hispanic — that you, with the probable help of the corporate bullies, have discouraged with your hand-picked gay, rich golden boy." (The "corporate bullies" are those Charlotte business leaders who protested the board's arts funding cuts.)

The chairman defended his support of the candidate: "He is an articulate, thoughtful, committed person who represents the Hispanic community. I did not ask him about his sexuality; it was not relevant to me." The candidate was not running on any "gay agenda" as the right-wing commissioner claimed. "This is just an example of bigotry and hate, and I don't believe that's truly what God wants," the gay candidate said.

The conservative commissioner wrote in a letter to the chairman: "What some of our corporate leaders and many other Americans fail to understand, including you, is that tolerance is good when defined to oppose racial, gender, ethnic and/or religious bigotry. However, when tolerance is expanded to include the acceptance of sexually deviant behavior, including the seducing of naive adults and children and the abandonment of moral standards, it is time to become intolerant....The homosexual agenda is part of a broad cultural transformation which seeks to make Charlotte the Sodom and Gomorrah capital of the east coast...."

The chairman's conservative critic joined with the board's Republican minority to vote in a new Republican chairman. The conservative Democrat was elected vice chair. The new chairman asked the board of commissioners to "no longer discuss homosexuality, diversity or other issues" that caused bitter division among the board. "[W]e must keep these debates in perspective," he said, "and realize that they are and should be lower priorities as we consider the more serious issues."

OHIO

In October, a unanimous panel of the United States Court of Appeals for the Sixth Circuit upheld **Cincinnati, Ohio's** controversial anti-gay rights charter amendment, Issue 3, which barred specific protection for gay men, lesbians, and bisexuals.

After its ruling in *Romer v. Evans* against Colorado's similarly-worded anti-gay Amendment 2 — holding that the amendment violated the U.S. Constitution's equal protection provisions by singling out gay men, lesbians and bisexuals for discriminatory treatment — the United States Supreme Court vacated the original 1995 decision by the three-judge panel upholding Cincinnati's charter amendment. The Court sent the Cincinnati case back to the Sixth Circuit for reconsideration in light of the holding in *Romer*. Despite *Romer*, the Sixth Circuit panel again upheld Issue 3.

The Sixth Circuit's most recent decision leaves Cincinnati as the only city in the country with an anti-gay law of this type. That law, like the Colorado initiative struck down by the Supreme Court, repealed city laws and policies banning discrimination based on sexual orientation and prohibited any future laws and policies from being enacted. The major force behind Colorado's anti-gay Amendment 2, Colorado for Family Values, reportedly provided 76 percent of the money ($390,000) that fueled Cincinnati's 1993 Issue 3 campaign.

An attorney for the Lambda Legal Defense and Education Fund, which filed a rehearing petition before the full Sixth Circuit, said that "Issue 3 is cut from the same despicable cloth as Colorado's Amendment 2..." "The ...decision upholding Issue 3 conflicts squarely with the Supreme Court's decision in *Romer*," said another Lambda attorney.

And an associate professor at the Georgetown University Law Center remarked, "This is a court that is looking at the trees and is completely missing the forest. It focuses on details that may seem important and misses the principal point of the Supreme Court's decision, (which is) that government may not take action against a group solely because other people dislike the group."

The petition for rehearing was denied, leaving the anti-gay law in effect. Issue 3 opponents have again asked the Supreme Court to hear the case.

The decision to hold a park-sanctioned "gay day" at an **Ohio** amusement park received unexpected approval from a national Religious Right group. Lesbians, gay men, bisexuals and their supporters have held an informal "gay day" at Paramount's Kings Island for the past thirteen years. This year, park officials offered the Gay and Lesbian Community Center of Greater **Cincinnati** exclusive after-hours access to the park in September. Kings Island offers similar private parties to major corporations.

Unusual support for the decision came from the anti-gay Christian Family Network (CFN). "By holding a Gay Day at the time when the general public is not present," the president of CFN said, "...families are safe from unwanted, unsolicited subjection to homosexuality activity." The amusement park had received complaints in previous years over displays of same-sex affection and what CFN labeled "in-your-face homosexuality."

The Christian Family Network is part of a national boycott of the Walt Disney Co. over issues including similar "gay day" festivities at company theme parks.

OREGON

The **Oregon** Citizens Alliance is collecting signatures for a ballot measure that would define "family" for governmental purposes as the union between a man and a woman. Such language would prohibit same-sex marriage in Oregon and prevent state and local governments from providing domestic benefits for same-sex partners.

In October, the Oregon attorney general certified a state ballot initiative prohibiting employment discrimination based on sexual orientation. Gay and lesbian activists have until July 1998 to secure 73,261 valid voter signatures for the November 1998 general election ballot. Activists had been working since the beginning of 1997 on the wording of the job-discrimination initiative. "I hope they make it," Lon Mabon, executive director of the Oregon Citizens Alliance said. "We can have a basic up or down vote" on the issue of gay rights. "The only way to stop the agenda of the homosexual community is to actually defeat them," he stated.

PENNSYLVANIA

A gay bar in rural **Somerset County, Pennsylvania** became the target of community outrage, protests and picketing by the Ku Klux Klan and local fundamentalists.

The heterosexual couple who own the business converted the roadside restaurant to a gay bar early in 1997. More than 50 area residents packed a town meeting and demanded that town supervisors close the establishment. Town officials said they had no legal authority to do so as the owners had all the proper permits and were operating the bar as a legal business.

At the meeting, angry townspeople claimed pornographic materials were being left on their front lawns and a flier allegedly advertising sexual activity at the bar had been distributed to their mailboxes. In fact, a discount drink notice from the club announcing a one-night "blowout" had been altered to "blow job" and re-distributed. The owners expressed the view that the flier and cache of pornographic materials were "obviously done by people trying to make us look bad."

Members of a local church began heckling and harassing patrons at the bar. The evangelical group began picketing the gay bar, carrying placards and signs that read: "HONK to close this gay bar" and "God Almighty hates sodomites."

In March, someone fired two shotgun blasts into the front door of the club. Two patrons received

"In the Sixties, we sat idly by and let prayer be removed from our schools. Now we are looking at the gay community coming into our community. I'm not willing to sit idly by."

Baptist minister in Myrtle Beach, South Carolina, objecting to a local gay pride event

minor injuries from flying glass and debris. Two months later, approximately 30 members of the Ku Klux Klan picketed outside the gay bar. The KKK protesters then relocated a mile down the road and burned three crosses. The club also received a bomb threat; no explosive was found.

The gay club remains open although it is the continued target of anti-gay pickets. Protesters have taken to videotaping patrons entering and leaving the club.

SOUTH CAROLINA

The mayor of **Myrtle Beach, South Carolina** joined local business and religious leaders in attacking a statewide gay group and its plans for an April 1998 pride festival. Organizers had chosen the city because the mayor, then a city councilman, had protested a gay bar opening in downtown Myrtle Beach.

Local real estate developers pressured businesses that had contracted to participate in the pride festival to withdraw their support. The developers, owners of a beachfront restaurant and entertainment complex, did not want their tenants linked to activities that endangered the "traditional family values" on which the company was based. A spokesman said, "We have nothing against these people as individuals, but this is a family-oriented environment, and we do not believe that bringing in that type of activity is in keeping with our wholesome family goals." The developers blocked one tenant from sponsoring a pride festival concert.

A local Baptist minister announced a counter march to the pride festival: "In the Sixties, we sat idly by and let prayer be removed from our schools. Now we are looking at the gay community coming into our community. I'm not willing to sit idly by," the minister said. "They are trying to impose a way of life on us with this festival that is probably already here but is just not flaunted. I don't see what this festival will accomplish except to create division."

The mayor entered the fray as the only council member to vote against closing city streets to accommodate the pride festival. He expressed concern that allowing gay men and lesbians to parade through the streets would set a dangerous precedent and would encourage Black Panthers, white supremacist skinheads and other extremist groups to stage similar marches. "[The mayor] is very callous and out of step with the facts of history in his remarks relating gays to skinheads and the Black Panthers," the president of the local NAACP chapter complained. "[T]hese groups have different agendas."

A local group established to oppose the pride festival, Concerned Citizens for Traditional Family Values, applauded the mayor's "tremendous stance for decency and traditional family values." Around 1,100 people attended a Traditional Family Values rally day prior to the pride festivities with speakers including the mayor, South Carolina lieutenant governor, the president of the Carolina Family Association and "ex-gay" Michael Johnston, president of Kerusso Ministries and founder of National Coming Out of Homosexuality Day.

The real estate developers who were among the first to protest the gay pride events in Myrtle Beach, dropped their slogan, "Boldly Shaping the Future with Pride," because "some people started using the word 'pride' a whole lot in our community," the company president and CEO said, referring to festival supporters.

The pride festival — with 5,000 attendees by police estimate — came off without further incident.

TEXAS

Two former employees of the **Texas** governor's office filed a lawsuit in **Austin** alleging that their former supervisor used hostile language to describe victims assistance programs for homosexuals.

The women were fired from the governor's Criminal Justice Division after complaining about abusive language and attitudes toward gays and lesbians by the division's executive director. They claimed the director had described victims assistance programs as "homo projects." The suit further alleged that the director wanted to track the number of crime victims who were gay and threatened to retaliate against grant applicants who complained about budget cuts.

The governor's office said, "The lawsuit is totally without merit."

A conference of Jewish lesbians, gay men and bisexuals held in **Dallas, Texas** was picketed by a handful of anti-gay protesters. Pickets from the east Texas-based "God Against Perversion" carried signs reading "Fag star not kosher" and "God hates fags" outside the 15th World Conference of Gay, Lesbian and Bisexual Jews.

The protest leader said he and his fellow pickets were following a biblical command. "The Bible said warn them, and whether they repent is not on my back," the Baptist pastor told a local television station. "I have to tell them."

VIRGINIA

A **Norfolk, Virginia** gay couple were the target of two fires — one, a confirmed arson — and an inflammatory, anti-gay letter mailed to their neighbors.

The couple returned home from a weekend trip to find the bed of their pick-up truck charred and burned. Norfolk police confirmed the incident as arson. After discussing the truck fire with a neighbor, the gay men discovered that an anonymous anti-gay letter had been mailed to their neighbors earlier in the year:

"This is to provide you some information about two of your newer neighbors. They have a long and violent history that you should be aware of before you or your loved ones come to harm. [The men] have had numerous arrests for such acts as molestation, deviant sexual practices, assault, resisting arrest, suspicion of burglary and arson, posession [sic] of drugs and assaulting an Officer. Those of you with children need to be aware of their love of the perverted, demented lifestyle. You should see that your children do not play around their house or accept candy or money from them. Please take notice and don't allow them to ruin any more lives like they have been doing for years."

Mere days after returning home to the burned pick-up, the couple were awakened one night to find that both their car and the truck were on fire.

The Norfolk police department is investigating any possible connections between the letter and the fires. The possibility of a hate crime has not been ruled out, but the fires are only being investigated as arson. "Arson cases sometimes take over a year to solve...we want to build a solid case so that we can prosecute and convict," a police spokesman said.

WASHINGTON

An ongoing battle between gay rights proponents and Christian conservatives on the **Kitsap County, Washington** Council on Human Rights led to the resignation of four of its 12 members. The Human Rights Council was formed to advise county commissioners on "issues related to discrimination, violence and harassment based on race, national origin, religion, gender, sexual orientation, physical handicap or economic status."

Tensions grew after the mayor appointed two anti-gay crusaders to the board. One outspoken conservative member tried to block council sponsorship of a play that suggested that homosexuality is not abnormal and denounced a gay citizen who routinely testified before the board. The council member said he and his family were harassed because of his views and accused liberal council members of plotting to depose him for his religious beliefs.

The state Christian Coalition publicly supported him and its executive director wrote to the county commissioners: "Some older board members project the attitude that this board exists for the personal agenda of homosexual(s) and other disaffected members of the community. The thought that heterosexual Christians have something to offer in the area of Human Rights...appears to be foreign to many of your members and supporters."

"We would not want a parade for thieves or people who rob banks or a parade for adulterers, homosexuals or lesbian lifestyles. It is wrong, I believe, to parade sin."

Baptist minister in Asheville, North Carolina, objecting to a local gay pride march

The four members who resigned plan to form a non-profit group dedicated to fighting bias. A county commissioner suggested disbanding the original human rights council. "We could do away with it," the commissioner said.

"I'm not sure that's the answer, but we have to rethink its mission, how it conducts business and who's on it."

Hate crimes in Kitsap County increased in 1997 while they decreased statewide.

A gay couple claimed their arrest outside a **Puyallup, Washington** fair was "malicious harassment." Police had arrested the men on charges of "disorderly conduct" and "resisting arrest."

Officers reported that they had received complaints about the men's appearance. They were wearing leather chaps with swimming trucks underneath and T-shirts, apparel considered legal in the state of Washington. The officers asked them to leave. After the couple left the fairgrounds, an unidentified man began yelling anti-gay slurs at them. One of the gay men responded with an obscene gesture. Reportedly, a policeman then "attacked" the gay man, pulling him to the ground while another officer repeatedly sprayed mace in the gay man's eyes and mouth. The officers arrested him and his partner, holding them at the Puyallup Municipal Jail for 12 hours.

The couple said they intend to press malicious harassment charges against the officers they claim assaulted them.

Lesbian and gay employees of **Seattle, Washington** were enraged by a city civil rights official's ruling allowing an anti-gay crusader to attend the meetings of their gay and lesbian employees' organization. The director of the Seattle Office for Civil Rights (OCR) ruled that the head of a local anti-gay group, known for his confrontational tactics in disrupting gay community events, could attend meetings of Seattle Employees Association for Gays and Lesbians (SEAGL). The organization had barred the conservative city employee and leader of the anti-gay Family Values Coalition from attending its meetings. The man had demanded copies of sign-in sheets with city employees' home addresses and phone numbers and had disrupted meetings. The city's Human Rights Department had dismissed several previous complaints of harassment by the anti-gay activist. In 1990, he filed a complaint about being barred from SEAGL meetings, which led to the recent ruling in his favor. "His whole purpose was to harass and intimidate gay city employees," a lesbian city employee stated.

The OCR director also ordered that SEAGL members undergo sensitivity training "including a discussion of [the complainant's] protected class." The director awarded the anti-gay activist $1,000 "for pain and suffering" and $1,864 to his attorneys, the conservative Rutherford Institute.

SEAGL expressed disappointment over the ruling. "The purpose and intent and spirit of laws like the city of Seattle's ordinances is to assure that people who have historically been victims of discrimination are protected from intimidation, harassment and unwelcome treatment solely because of sexual orientation, age, race, sex, and other factors over which we have no control," a coordinator for SEAGL said. "It is deeply troubling and ironic to members of SEAGL that the City of Seattle Office for Civil Rights, by this ruling, may be giving legal sanction to individuals to engage in such behavior against the various individuals the law was designed to protect." Gay and lesbian employees are concerned that the presence of opponents at their meetings will curtail their ability to speak freely on sensitive issues, will lead to harassment of the opponent's gay co-workers, and they fear that attempts will be made to disrupt their private lives.

"This is a very bad decision that we need to get overturned," said the chair of another gay and lesbian city employees group. "What is this? The OCR orders gay employees to undergo sensitivity training to understand why anti-gay activists are a protected class? The OCR awarded him $1,000 for pain and suffering!"

SEAGL's leadership is considering removing the group from city-employee-organization status to avoid future problems and is also investigating an appeal to the ruling.

Conservative talk show host Michael Medved lambasted the **Seattle, Washington** gay community in a July radio broadcast. Medved had secured a copy of the community phonebook of the Greater Seattle Business Association (GSBA), the local gay business owner's organization, and used an hour of his air time for an anti-gay diatribe against the organizations and services listed in the directory.

Medved labeled Ubiquitous, a mentoring organization providing a safe environment for adolescents and adults to interact, as "a place where adults get to hit on teenaged boys." During his broadcast, Medved called the GSBA scholarship program — "which clearly encourages students to identify themselves as gay or lesbian" — an attempt to recruit students into "the gay lifestyle," and described the Sisters of Perpetual Indulgence, a drag AIDS fundraising group, as "the flaming nuns."

Medved attempted to discredit anti-discrimination legislation. "Look at their directory and tell me we're dealing with an oppressed minority," Medved railed. "Part of the whole idea behind the gay rights referendum Initiative 677 that will be on the ballot in the state of Washington is that gay people have been kept down. They can't get ahead... Look at all their businesses! They're bankers and dentists and doctors! This is not a community that shows evidence of being ground into the dust, of being hopelessly oppressed. Quite the contrary."

Medved urged listeners to join the anti-gay Washington Family Council, the state affiliate of Focus on the Family.

WISCONSIN

A group of protesters marched outside an **Eau Claire, Wisconsin** high school with anti-gay placards. Members of Wisconsin Christians United carried picket signs that read "Homosexuals — Repent or Perish" and passed out pamphlets entitled "Do Homosexuals Spend Eternity in Heaven or Hell." The same protesters had picketed the previous day with anti-abortion signs, but had been ignored.

The group's leader explained "these young people have the right to hear the other side of this argument."

A gay student said the protesters were "teaching hate and revenge."

A **Madison, Wisconsin** firefighter, appealing his suspension for distributing anti-gay brochures at work, was featured in two prominent conservative publications. The man, who is also a local preacher, had been suspended from the Fire Department last year for two months without pay for distributing a biblical tract, "The Truth About Homosexuality," and for making intemperate remarks to a reporter about the fire chief.

The firefighter was featured in a Family Research Council publication, *The Other Side of Tolerance*, and appeared on the cover of the conservative magazine *World*, gagged by a rainbow flag. The right-wing press characterized his plight as a free speech and religious freedom issue. The *World* article, "Zero Tolerance," also made coy references to the Madison fire chief's sexual orientation, noting that, "while she has refused to comment publicly about her sexual habits, [she] has strong, visible ties to the homosexual community" and was a drummer in an all-woman band "that played the lesbian bookstore circuit." "Zero Tolerance" reported on a 1996 protest at the man's church without mentioning that the main speaker was the controversial Scott Lively, author of *The Pink Swastika*, who disputes the fact that gay men and lesbians were Holocaust victims and claims that they were influential in the Nazi party.

The anti-gay firefighter was also the guest of honor at a rally for biblical morality and marriage sponsored by the anti-gay Wisconsin Christians United, where he was portrayed as a Christian being persecuted for his faith by the "People's Republic" or "Soviet Socialist Republic of Madison." He urged the crowd to "stand up and speak out... Because if you don't stand up, you and your household will perish amidst all this evil and wickedness," he said.

During the firefighter's appeal before the Police and Fire Commission, the city attorney called him a "chronic malcontent" with a "very checkered disciplinary record." The man had been charged with insubordination before and suspended without pay for 18 hours and two weeks in two previous disciplinary cases.

The firefighter's attorney argued that if publications such as *Penthouse, Sports Illustrated, Popular Mechanics* and the local gay newspaper were allowed in the firehouse, a tract about the Bible should also be allowed. The attorney noted the man's record of achievement of mediation between the fire department and the black community.

The Madison Police and Fire Commission decided in June that the firefighter's distribution of the pamphlet violated department policy against workplace harassment. The firefighter and his attorney are appealing the decision.

The firefighter, now facing permanent termination from the department, has lobbied Congress on behalf of the anti-gay Traditional Values Coalition, urging legislators to reject the Employment Non-Discrimination Act (ENDA), proposed federal employment protection for lesbians and gay men.

Anti-gay pickets protested outside a **Milwaukee, Wisconsin** hotel, host to an anniversary celebration for the state's gay newspaper. Members of Wisconsin Christians United and the Christian Civil Liberties Union carried picket signs and handed out anti-gay pamphlets.

"Homosexuality is a vile perversion that if we leave unchecked will bring the downfall of the nation," the founder of Wisconsin Christians United later proclaimed at a group-sponsored rally for Biblical morality and marriage. "Homosexual marriage violates God's law. We need to outlaw homosexual activities in the state and enforce that law."

ACKNOWLEDGEMENTS

People For the American Way Foundation would like to acknowledge the activists and organizations around the country who are working to improve the climate for gay men and lesbians, and who provided us with information for this edition of *Hostile Climate.*

In particular, we would like to thank the following organizations and their staffs for their continuing assistance:

American Civil Liberties Union

D.C. Metro Area Safe Schools Coalition

Federation of Statewide LGBT Political Organizations

Freedom to Marry Coalition

Gay, Lesbian and Straight Education Network

Gay and Lesbian Alliance Against Defamation

Gay and Lesbian Victory Fund

Human Rights Campaign

Lambda Legal Defense and Education Fund

LIFE: California's Lesbian/Gay and AIDS Lobby and Institute

Log Cabin Republicans

L.A. Gay and Lesbian Center

Montana Human Rights Network

National Black Lesbian and Gay Leadership Forum

National Center for Lesbian Rights

National Coalition of Anti-Violence Programs

National Gay and Lesbian Task Force

National Youth Advocacy Coalition

Parents, Families and Friends of Lesbians and Gays

P.E.R.S.O.N. (Public Education Regarding Sexual Orientation) Project

Servicemembers Legal Defense Network

Triangle Foundation

STATE-BY-STATE INCIDENT INDEX

PEOPLE FOR THE AMERICAN WAY FOUNDATION'S
HOSTILE CLIMATE TEAM

Lead Researcher
JS (Jim) Adams

The Andrew Heiskell Library
Erica Lasdon
Christine Lenschow

Director, Education Policy/Research Manager
Deanna Duby

Research and Writing Assistance
Kevin Althouse
Matthew Freeman
Jeffrey Porro

Production
Will Heyniger
Delisa Saunders

Design
Supon Design Group

People For the American Way Foundation
2000 M Street NW — Suite 400
Washington, DC 20036
1 800-326-PFAW
pfaw@pfaw.org / www.pfaw.org